THE COMPLETE JUICING RECIPE BOOK FOR BEGINNERS

The Essential Guide of Juicing Recipes to Reduce Body Fat, Boost Energy, Fight Disease, and Live Long

Diana W. Dorris

TABLE OF CONTENT

1.STRAWBERRY DELIGHT

Time: 5 mins

Servings: 1

INGREDIENTS:

- 1 cup of strawberries, hulled and split
- 1/2 cup of coconut milk
- 1/2 cup of orange juice
- 1 tbsp honey
- Ice cubes

INSTRUCTIONS:

1. Strawberries, coconut milk, orange juice, honey, and a few ice cubes Must all be blended together.

2. Blend till creamy and smooth.

3. The Strawberry Delight Must be poured into a cold glass and served.

NUTRITION INFO (PER SERVING):

Cals: 120

Carbs: 26g

Fat: 4g

Protein: 2g

2. MELON MINGLE

Time: 10 mins

Servings: 2

INGREDIENTS:

- 2 cups of cubed watermelon
- 1 cup of cubed honeydew melon
- 1 cup of cubed cantaloupe
- Juice of 1 lime
- 1 tbsp agave syrup
- Fresh mint leaves (for garnish)

INSTRUCTIONS:

1. Watermelon, honeydew melon, cantaloupe, lime juice, and agave syrup Must all be mixd in a blender.

2. Up to smooth, blend.

3. Add fresh mint leaves as a garnish after pouring the Melon Mingle into glasses.

4. Offer cold.

NUTRITION INFO (PER SERVING):

Cals: 80

Carbs: 20g

Fat: 0g

Protein: 1g

3.GOLDEN GODDESS

Time: 20 mins

Servings: 2

INGREDIENTS:

- 2 ripe bananas
- 1 cup of pineapple chunks
- 1 cup of mango chunks
- 1 tbsp turmeric powder
- 1 cup of coconut milk
- 1 tbsp honey (non-compulsory)
- Ice cubes

INSTRUCTIONS:

1. Put the ripe bananas, mango, pineapple, turmeric powder, coconut milk, and honey (if using) in a blender.

2. Blend till creamy and smooth.

3. When the mixture is cold and foamy, add ice cubes and mix once more.

4. Pour into glasses and start serving right away.

NUTRITION INFO (PER SERVING):

Cals: 250

Protein: 3g

Fat: 6g

Carbs: 50g

Fiber: 5g

4.MINTY MELODY

Time: 10 mins

Servings: 1

INGREDIENTS:

- 1 cup of fresh spinach
- 1 cup of pineapple chunks
- 1 ripe banana
- 1/2 cup of fresh mint leaves
- 1 cup of coconut water
- Ice cubes

INSTRUCTIONS:

1. Blend together the coconut water, fresh mint leaves, ripe banana, pineapple pieces, and fresh spinach.

2. Blend till creamy and smooth.

3. When the mixture is cold and foamy, add ice cubes and mix once more.

4. Add a sprig of fresh mint as a garnish after pouring into a glass.

NUTRITION INFO (PER SERVING):

Cals: 180

Protein: 3g

Fat: 1g

Carbs: 45g

Fiber: 6g

5.GREEN SYMPHONY

Time: 15 mins

Servings: 2

INGREDIENTS:

- 2 cups of baby spinach
- 1 ripe avocado
- 1 green apple, cored and chop-up
- 1 cup of cucumber slices
- 1 cup of coconut water
- Juice of 1 lime
- Ice cubes

INSTRUCTIONS:

1. Baby spinach, ripe avocado, green apple, cucumber slices, coconut water, and lime juice Must all be mixd in a blender.

2. Blend till creamy and smooth.

3. When the mixture is cold and foamy, add ice cubes and mix once more.

4. Pour into glasses and start serving right away.

NUTRITION INFO (PER SERVING):

Cals: 220

Protein: 4g

Fat: 10g

Carbs: 30g

Fiber: 10g

6.BERRY BLISS

Time: 10 mins

Servings: 1

INGREDIENTS:

- 1 cup of combined berries (strawberries, blueberries, raspberries)
- 1 ripe banana
- 1 cup of almond milk
- 1 tbsp honey (non-compulsory)
- Ice cubes

INSTRUCTIONS:

1. Blend together the almond milk, combined berries, ripe banana, and honey (if using).

2. Blend till creamy and smooth.

3. When the mixture is cold and foamy, add ice cubes and mix once more.

4. Place in a glass and sip.

NUTRITION INFO (PER SERVING):

Cals: 180

Protein: 3g

Fat: 2g

Carbs: 40g

Fiber: 8g

7.CITRUS SPLASH

Time: 5 mins

Servings: 1

INGREDIENTS:

- 1 orange, peel off and segmented
- 1 grapefruit, peel off and segmented
- 1 lemon, juiced
- 1 lime, juiced
- 1 cup of coconut water
- Ice cubes

INSTRUCTIONS:

1. Orange, grapefruit, and lime segments, coconut water, and their juices Must all be mixd in a blender.

2. Blend everything thoroughly up to it's smooth.

3. one you've added the ice cubes, mix the liquid one more to chill it.

4. Pour into a glass, then serve right away.

NUTRITION INFO (PER SERVING):

Cals: 90

Protein: 1g

Fat: 0g

Carbs: 22g

Fiber: 3g

8. VEGGIE WONDER

Time: 15 mins

Servings: 2

INGREDIENTS:

- 2 carrots, peel off and chop-up
- 1 cup of baby spinach
- 1 cucumber, peel off and chop-up
- 1 stalk celery, chop-up
- 1 cup of coconut water
- Juice of 1 lemon
- Ice cubes

INSTRUCTIONS:

1. Blend the carrots, baby spinach, cucumber, celery, coconut water, and lemon juice together in a blender.

2. Blend everything thoroughly up to it's smooth.

3. one you've added the ice cubes, mix the liquid one more to chill it.

4. Pour into glasses and start serving right away.

NUTRITION INFO (PER SERVING):

Cals: 90

Protein: 2g

Fat: 1g

Carbs: 20g

Fiber: 4g

9.POWER POTION

Time: 10 mins

Servings: 1

INGREDIENTS:

- 1 cup of kale leaves
- 1 cup of spinach leaves
- 1/2 cucumber, peel off and chop-up
- 1/2 green apple, cored and chop-up
- 1 tbsp chia seeds
- 1 cup of coconut water
- Ice cubes

INSTRUCTIONS:

1. In a blender, mix the kale, spinach, cucumber, green apple, chia seeds, and coconut water.

2. Blend everything thoroughly up to it's smooth.

3. one you've added the ice cubes, mix the liquid one more to chill it.

4. Place in a glass and sip.

NUTRITION INFO (PER SERVING):

Cals: 120

Protein: 5g

Fat: 3g

Carbs: 25g

Fiber: 8g

10. RAINBOW DELIGHT

Time: 15 mins

Servings: 2

INGREDIENTS:

- 1 cup of strawberries, hulled and split
- 1 cup of pineapple chunks
- 1 cup of spinach leaves
- 1 banana
- 1 cup of almond milk
- Ice cubes

INSTRUCTIONS:

1. Blend the strawberries, pineapple pieces, spinach leaves, banana, and almond milk together in a blender.

2. Blend everything thoroughly up to it's smooth.

3. one you've added the ice cubes, mix the liquid one more to chill it.

4. Pour into glasses and start serving right away.

NUTRITION INFO (PER SERVING):

Cals: 150

Protein: 3g

Fat: 2g

Carbs: 35g

Fiber: 6g

11.LEMON LIME DELIGHT

Time: 5 mins

Servings: 1

INGREDIENTS:

- Juice of 1 lemon
- Juice of 1 lime
- 1 tbsp honey (non-compulsory)
- 1 cup of water
- Ice cubes

INSTRUCTIONS:

1. Lemon juice, lime juice, honey (if preferred), and water Must all be mixd in a glass.

2. Up to the honey is dissolved, stir thoroughly.

3. Re-stir, then add the ice cubes.

4. Serve right away.

NUTRITION INFO (PER SERVING):

Cals: 30

Protein: 0g

Fat: 0g

Carbs: 9g

Fiber: 0g

12.ORANGE ZEST

Time: 10 mins

Servings: 1

INGREDIENTS:

- 1 orange, peel off and segmented
- 1 carrot, peel off and chop-up
- 1/2-inch piece of ginger, peel off
- 1 cup of orange juice
- Ice cubes

INSTRUCTIONS:

1. Orange juice, diced carrot, peel off ginger, and orange segment pieces Must all be mixd in a blender.

2. Blend everything thoroughly up to it's smooth.

3. one you've added the ice cubes, mix the liquid one more to chill it.

4. Place in a glass and sip.

NUTRITION INFO (PER SERVING):

Cals: 100

Protein: 2g

Fat: 1g

Carbs: 24g

Fiber: 4g

13. GREEN GODDESS

Time: 5 mins

Servings: 1

INGREDIENTS:

- 1 cup of spinach
- 1/2 avocado
- 1/2 cucumber
- 1/2 lemon, juiced
- 1 tbsp fresh parsley
- 1 cup of coconut water

INSTRUCTIONS:

1. Blend the spinach, avocado, cucumber, lemon juice, parsley, and coconut water in a food processor.

2. Blend till creamy and smooth.

3. Pour cold liquid into a glass and serve.

NUTRITION INFO (PER SERVING):

Cals: 150

Protein: 5g

Fat: 10g

Carbs: 15g

Fiber: 7g

14. BERRY BLAST

Time: 5 mins

Servings: 1

INGREDIENTS:

- 1 cup of combined berries (strawberries, blueberries, raspberries)
- 1/2 banana
- 1 cup of almond milk
- 1 tbsp honey or maple syrup (non-compulsory)

INSTRUCTIONS:

1. In a blender, mix the combined berries, banana, almond milk, and sweetener (if using).

2. Blend everything thoroughly up to it's smooth.

3. Place in a glass and sip.

NUTRITION INFO (PER SERVING):

Cals: 180

Protein: 2g

Fat: 3g

Carbs: 40g

Fiber: 7g

15.TROPICAL PARADISE

Time: 5 mins

Servings: 1

INGREDIENTS:

- 1/2 cup of pineapple chunks
- 1/2 cup of mango chunks
- 1/2 banana
- 1 cup of coconut water

INSTRUCTIONS:

1. Blend the banana, mango, pineapple, and coconut water in a food processor.

2. Blend till creamy and smooth.

3. Pour cold liquid into a glass and serve.

NUTRITION INFO (PER SERVING):

Cals: 150

Protein: 2g

Fat: 1g

Carbs: 35g

Fiber: 5g

16. CITRUS SUNRISE

Time: 5 mins

Servings: 1

INGREDIENTS:

- 1 orange, peel off and segmented
- 1/2 grapefruit, peel off and segmented
- 1/2 lemon, juiced
- 1/2 lime, juiced
- 1 cup of water

INSTRUCTIONS:

1. Blend the water, lemon, lime, orange, and grapefruit segments, as well as the juices in a blender.

2. Blend everything thoroughly up to it's smooth.

3. Pour cold liquid into a glass and serve.

NUTRITION INFO (PER SERVING):

Cals: 80

Protein: 2g

Fat: 0g

Carbs: 20g

Fiber: 4g

17. CUCUMBER COOLER

Time: 5 mins

Servings: 1

INGREDIENTS:

- 1 cucumber
- 1/2 lime, juiced
- 1 tbsp fresh mint leaves
- 1 cup of water

INSTRUCTIONS:

1. Slice the cucumber into mini bits after peeling.

2. In a blender, mix the cucumber chunks, lime juice, mint leaves, and water.

3. Blend everything thoroughly up to it's smooth.

4. Pour cold liquid into a glass and serve.

NUTRITION INFO (PER SERVING):

Cals: 30

Protein: 1g

Fat: 0g

Carbs: 8g

Fiber: 2g

18. APPLE ZINGER

Time: 5 mins

Servings: 1

INGREDIENTS:

- 1 apple, cored and chop-up
- 1/2 inch fresh ginger, peel off
- 1/2 lemon, juiced
- 1 cup of water

INSTRUCTIONS:

1. In a blender, mix the apple pieces, ginger, lemon juice, and water.

2. Blend everything thoroughly up to it's smooth.

3. Pour cold liquid into a glass and serve.

NUTRITION INFO (PER SERVING):

Cals: 60

Protein: 1g

Fat: 0g

Carbs: 15g

Fiber: 3g

19.CARROT CRUNCH

Time: 5 mins

Servings: 1

INGREDIENTS:

- 1 carrot, peel off and chop-up
- 1/2 orange, peel off and segmented
- 1/2 apple, cored and chop-up
- 1/2 inch fresh ginger, peel off
- 1 cup of water

INSTRUCTIONS:

1. In a blender, mix the carrot, apple chunks, orange segments, ginger, and water.

2. Blend everything thoroughly up to it's smooth.

3. Pour cold liquid into a glass and serve.

NUTRITION INFO (PER SERVING):

Cals: 70

Protein: 1g

Fat: 0g

Carbs: 18g

Fiber: 4g

20.BEET BLAST

Time: 5 mins

Servings: 1

INGREDIENTS:

- 1 mini beet, peel off and chop-up
- 1/2 cup of strawberries
- 1/2 cup of raspberries
- 1/2 cup of coconut water

INSTRUCTIONS:

1. Blend the coconut water, strawberries, raspberries, and beet in a blender.

2. Blend everything thoroughly up to it's smooth.

3. Pour cold liquid into a glass and serve.

NUTRITION INFO (PER SERVING):

Cals: 120

Protein: 3g

Fat: 1g

Carbs: 27g

Fiber: 9g

21.PINEAPPLE PUNCH

Time: 5 mins

Servings: 1

INGREDIENTS:

- 1 cup of pineapple chunks
- 1/2 cup of orange juice
- 1/2 cup of coconut milk

INSTRUCTIONS:

1. In a blender, mix the pineapple pieces, orange juice, and coconut milk.

2. Blend everything thoroughly up to it's smooth.

3. Pour cold liquid into a glass and serve.

NUTRITION INFO (PER SERVING):

Cals: 180

Protein: 2g

Fat: 6g

Carbs: 35g

Fiber: 2g

22.MANGO MADNESS

Time: 5 mins

Servings: 1

INGREDIENTS:

- 1 cup of mango chunks
- 1/2 cup of orange juice
- 1/2 cup of almond milk

INSTRUCTIONS:

1. In a blender, mix the mango pieces, orange juice, and almond milk.

2. Blend everything thoroughly up to it's smooth.

3. Pour cold liquid into a glass and serve.

NUTRITION INFO (PER SERVING):

Cals: 160

Protein: 2g

Fat: 3g

Carbs: 34g

Fiber: 3g

23.WATERMELON WONDER

Time: 10 mins

Servings: 2

INGREDIENTS:

- 4 cups of watermelon, diced
- Juice of 1 lime

- 1 cup of ice cubes

INSTRUCTIONS:

1. Watermelon, lime juice, and ice cubes Must all be mixd in a blender.
2. Up to smooth, blend.
3. Offer cold.

24.LEMON LIMEADE

Time: 15 mins

Servings: 4

INGREDIENTS:

- Juice of 4 lemons
- Juice of 4 limes
- 4 cups of water
- 1/4 cup of honey or sugar
- Ice cubes

INSTRUCTIONS:

1. Lemon juice, lime juice, water, and honey/sugar Must all be mixd in a pitcher.
2. Stir the honey/sugar mixture up to it dissolves.
3. Serve cooled after adding ice cubes.

25.KALE KICK

Time: 5 mins

Servings: 1

INGREDIENTS:

- 1 cup of kale leaves
- 1/2 cup of pineapple chunks
- 1/2 cup of coconut water

- 1 tbsp fresh ginger, finely grated

INSTRUCTIONS:

1. Kale leaves, pineapple chunks, coconut water, and finely grated ginger Must all be blended together.
2. Up to smooth, blend.
3. Enjoy right away.

26. SPINACH SURPRISE

Time: 8 mins

Servings: 2

INGREDIENTS:

- 2 cups of spinach leaves
- 1 cup of refrigerate mango chunks
- 1/2 cup of almond milk
- 1 tbsp chia seeds

INSTRUCTIONS:

1. Blend spinach leaves, mango chunks that have been refrigerate, almond milk, and chia seeds together in a blender.
2. Up to smooth, blend.
3. Offer cold.

27. GINGER SNAP

Time: 10 mins

Servings: 1

INGREDIENTS:

- 1 medium apple, cored and diced
- 1/2 inch fresh ginger, peel off and finely grated
- 1 cup of almond milk
- 1 tbsp honey or maple syrup
- Pinch of cinnamon (non-compulsory)

INSTRUCTIONS:

1. Apple, ginger, almond milk, honey or maple syrup, and cinnamon (if using) Must all be put in a blender.
2. Up to smooth, blend.
3. Place in a glass and sip.

28. POMEGRANATE PASSION

Time: 5 mins

Servings: 1

INGREDIENTS:

- 1 cup of pomegranate seeds
- 1/2 cup of coconut water
- Juice of 1 lime
- 1 tsp honey or agave syrup

INSTRUCTIONS:

1. Pomegranate seeds, coconut water, lime juice, and honey/agave syrup Must all be mixd in a blender.
2. Blend everything thoroughly.

3. Offer cold.

29. BLUEBERRY BLISS

Time: 5 mins

Servings: 1

INGREDIENTS:

- 1 cup of blueberries
- 1/2 cup of Greek yogurt
- 1/2 cup of almond milk
- 1 tbsp honey
- Ice cubes

INSTRUCTIONS:

1. Blend blueberries, Greek yogurt, almond milk, honey, and ice cubes together in a blender.
2. Up to smooth, blend.
3. Place in a glass and sip.

30. RASPBERRY REFRESHER

Time: 7 mins

Servings: 2

INGREDIENTS:

- 2 cups of raspberries
- 1 cup of coconut water
- Juice of 1 lemon
- 1 tbsp agave syrup or honey
- Mint leaves for garnish (non-compulsory)

INSTRUCTIONS:

1. Raspberries, coconut water, lemon juice, and agave syrup/honey Must all be mixd in a blender.
2. Blend everything thoroughly.
3. If preferred, garnish with mint leaves and serve cold.

31.ORANGE CREAMSICLE

Time: 5 mins

Servings: 1

INGREDIENTS:

- 1 Big orange, peel off and segmented
- 1/2 cup of coconut milk
- 1 tsp vanilla extract
- 1 tbsp honey or maple syrup
- Ice cubes

INSTRUCTIONS:

1. Orange segments, coconut milk, vanilla extract, honey or maple syrup, and ice cubes Must all be put in a blender.
2. Blend till creamy and smooth.
3. Place in a glass and sip.

32.KIWI QUENCHER

Time: 5 mins

Servings: 1

INGREDIENTS:

- 2 kiwis, peel off and split
- 1/2 cup of cucumber, peel off and chop-up
- 1/2 cup of coconut water
- Juice of 1 lime
- 1 tbsp honey or agave syrup
- Ice cubes

INSTRUCTIONS:

1. Kiwis, cucumber, coconut water, lime juice, honey or agave syrup, and ice cubes Must all be mixd in a blender.
2. Blend everything thoroughly.
3. Offer cold.

33.PEAR PERFECTION

Time: 7 mins

Servings: 2

INGREDIENTS:

- 2 ripe pears, peel off and diced
- 1 cup of spinach leaves
- 1/2 cup of almond milk
- 1 tbsp honey or maple syrup
- 1/2 tsp vanilla extract
- Ice cubes

1. Diced pears, spinach leaves, almond milk, honey or maple syrup, vanilla essence, and ice cubes Must all be mixd in a blender.
2. Up to smooth, blend.
3. Pour cold liquid into glasses and serve.

34. PEVERY DELIGHT

Time: 8 mins

Servings: 2

INGREDIENTS:

- 2 ripe peveryes, peel off and split
- 1/2 cup of Greek yogurt
- 1/2 cup of orange juice
- 1 tbsp honey or agave syrup
- Ice cubes

INSTRUCTIONS:

1. Split peveryes, Greek yogurt, orange juice, honey or agave syrup, and ice cubes Must all be mixd in a blender.
2. Blend up to incorporated and creamy.
3. Fill glasses with liquid and sip.

35. STRAWBERRY FIELDS

Time: 5 mins

Servings: 1

INGREDIENTS:

- 1 cup of strawberries, hulled and halved
- 1/2 cup of coconut water
- Juice of 1 lemon

- 1 tbsp honey or agave syrup
- Ice cubes

INSTRUCTIONS:

1. Strawberries, coconut water, lemon juice, honey or agave syrup, and ice cubes Must all be mixd in a blender.
2. Up to smooth, blend.
3. Pour cold liquid into a glass and serve.

36.MELON MEDLEY

Time: 10 mins

Servings: 2

INGREDIENTS:

- 2 cups of combined melons (watermelon, honeydew, cantaloupe), diced
- 1/2 cup of coconut water
- Juice of 1 lime
- 1 tbsp fresh mint leaves, chop-up
- Ice cubes

INSTRUCTIONS:

1. Mixture of melons, coconut water, lime juice, mint leaves, and ice cubes Must all be blended together.
2. Blend everything thoroughly.
3. Offer cold.

37. GOLDEN GLOW

Time: 5 mins

Servings: 1

INGREDIENTS:

- 1 medium carrot, peel off and chop-up
- 1 mini orange, peel off and segmented
- 1/2 inch fresh turmeric, peel off and finely grated
- 1/2 inch fresh ginger, peel off and finely grated
- 1 cup of coconut water
- Ice cubes

INSTRUCTIONS:

1. Blend the carrot, orange segments, ginger, turmeric, coconut water, and ice cubes in a blender.
2. Up to smooth, blend.
3. Place in a glass and sip.

38. REFRESHING MINT

Time: 5 mins

Servings: 1

INGREDIENTS:

- 1 cup of fresh mint leaves
- Juice of 1 lime
- 1 tbsp honey or agave syrup
- 2 cups of water
- Ice cubes

1. Mint leaves, lime juice, honey or agave syrup, water, and ice cubes Must all be blended together.
2. Blend everything thoroughly.
3. Filter the mixture to get rid of any remaining solids.
4. Pour cold liquid into a glass and serve.

39.ANTIOXIDANT POWERHOUSE

Time: 5 mins

Servings: 1

INGREDIENTS:

- 1 cup of combined berries (blueberries, strawberries, raspberries)
- 1/2 cup of pomegranate juice
- 1/2 cup of coconut water
- 1 tbsp chia seeds
- Ice cubes

INSTRUCTIONS:

1. Juice from a pomegranate, coconut water, chia seeds, and ice cubes Must all be mixd in a blender.
2. Up to smooth, blend.
3. Place in a glass and sip.

40. IMMUNE BOOSTER

Time: 5 mins

Servings: 1

INGREDIENTS:

- 1 medium orange, peel off and segmented
- 1/2 cup of pineapple chunks
- 1/2 cup of coconut water
- 1 tbsp fresh lemon juice
- 1 tsp honey or agave syrup
- Ice cubes

INSTRUCTIONS:

1. Orange segments, pineapple chunks, coconut water, lemon juice, honey/agave syrup, and ice cubes Must all be mixd in a blender.
2. Blend everything thoroughly.
3. Pour cold liquid into a glass and serve.

41. DIGESTIVE AID

Time: 5 mins

Servings: 1

INGREDIENTS:

- 1 cup of pineapple chunks
- 1/2 cup of cucumber, peel off and chop-up
- 1/2 cup of coconut water
- Juice of 1 lime
- 1 tbsp fresh mint leaves
- Ice cubes

INSTRUCTIONS:

1. Cucumber, coconut water, lime juice, pineapple chunks, fresh mint leaves, and ice cubes Must all be mixd in a blender.
2. Up to smooth, blend.
3. Place in a glass and sip.

42.ENERGIZING ELIXIR

Time: 5 mins

Servings: 1

INGREDIENTS:

- 1 cup of brewed green tea, cooled
- 1/2 cup of pineapple chunks
- 1/2 banana
- 1 tbsp honey or agave syrup
- Ice cubes

INSTRUCTIONS:

1. Blend brewed green tea with refrigerate pineapple, banana, honey or agave syrup, and ice cubes.
2. Blend everything thoroughly.
3. Pour cold liquid into a glass and serve.

43.SKIN SOOTHER

Time: 5 mins

Servings: 1

INGREDIENTS:

- 1 cup of cucumber, peel off and chop-up
- 1/2 cup of aloe vera juice
- Juice of 1 lemon
- 1 tbsp honey or agave syrup
- Ice cubes

INSTRUCTIONS:

1. Cucumber, aloe vera juice, lemon juice, honey/agave syrup, and ice cubes Must all be mixd in a blender.
2. Up to smooth, blend.
3. Place in a glass and sip.

44. DETOXIFYING CLEANSE

Time: 5 mins

Servings: 1

INGREDIENTS:

- 1 cup of kale leaves
- 1/2 cup of cucumber, peel off and chop-up
- 1/2 cup of coconut water
- Juice of 1 lemon
- 1 tbsp fresh parsley
- Ice cubes

INSTRUCTIONS:

1. Kale leaves, cucumber, coconut water, lemon juice, fresh parsley, and ice cubes Must all be mixd in a blender.
2. Blend everything thoroughly.
3. Pour cold liquid into a glass and serve.

45. STRESS RELIEVER

Time: 5 mins

Servings: 1

INGREDIENTS:

- 1 cup of chamomile tea, cooled
- 1/2 cup of mango chunks
- 1/2 banana
- 1 tbsp honey or agave syrup

- Ice cubes

INSTRUCTIONS:

1. Blend ice cubes, mango pieces, banana, honey or agave syrup, and chamomile tea together in a blender.
2. Up to smooth, blend.
3. Place in a glass and sip.

46. MOOD BOOSTER

Time: 5 mins

Servings: 1

INGREDIENTS:

- 1 cup of combined berries (strawberries, blueberries, raspberries)
- 1/2 cup of almond milk
- 1/2 cup of Greek yogurt
- 1 tbsp honey or agave syrup
- Ice cubes

INSTRUCTIONS:

1. Blend the combined berries, almond milk, Greek yogurt, honey or agave syrup, and ice cubes together in a blender.
2. Blend everything thoroughly.
3. Pour cold liquid into a glass and serve.

47. WEIGHT LOSS WONDER

Time: 5 mins

Servings: 1

INGREDIENTS:

- 1 cup of unsweetened almond milk
- 1/2 cup of refrigerate berries (blueberries, raspberries)
- 1/2 cup of spinach leaves

- 1 tbsp chia seeds
- 1 tsp honey or agave syrup
- Ice cubes

INSTRUCTIONS:

1. Almond milk, refrigerate berries, spinach leaves, chia seeds, honey or agave syrup, and ice cubes Must all be blended together.
2. Up to smooth, blend.
3. Place in a glass and sip.

48.HANGOVER HELPER

Time: 5 mins

Servings: 1

INGREDIENTS:

- 1 cup of coconut water
- 1/2 cup of pineapple chunks
- 1/2 cup of spinach leaves
- 1 tbsp fresh ginger, finely grated
- Juice of 1 lime
- Ice cubes

INSTRUCTIONS:

1. Coconut water, pineapple chunks, spinach leaves, finely grated ginger, lime juice, and ice cubes Must all be mixd in a blender.
2. Blend everything thoroughly.
3. Pour cold liquid into a glass and serve.

49. POST-WORKOUT REVIVER

Time: 5 mins

Servings: 1

INGREDIENTS:

- 1 cup of unsweetened almond milk
- 1/2 cup of refrigerate combined berries
- 1/2 banana
- 1 tbsp protein powder (vanilla or your preferred flavor)
- 1 tbsp almond butter
- Ice cubes

INSTRUCTIONS:

1. Almond milk, refrigerate combined berries, a banana, protein powder, almond butter, and ice cubes Must all be blended together.
2. Up to smooth, blend.
3. Place in a glass and sip.

50. SUMMER SIPPER

Time: 5 mins

Servings: 1

INGREDIENTS:

- 1 cup of watermelon, diced
- 1/2 cup of fresh strawberries
- 1/2 cup of coconut water
- Juice of 1 lime
- 1 tbsp fresh mint leaves
- Ice cubes

1. Watermelon, strawberries, coconut water, lime juice, mint leaves, and ice cubes Must all be mixd in a blender.
2. Up to smooth, blend.
3. Pour cold liquid into a glass and serve.

51.WINTER WARMER

Time: 10 mins

Servings: 2

INGREDIENTS:

- 2 cups of unsweetened almond milk
- 2 tbsp unsweetened cocoa powder
- 2 tbsp honey or maple syrup
- 1/2 tsp vanilla extract
- Pinch of cinnamon
- Pinch of nutmeg

INSTRUCTIONS:

1. Almond milk Must be heated in a pot to a warm but not boiling state.
2. Up to well blended, stir in the cocoa powder, honey or maple syrup, vanilla essence, cinnamon, and nutmeg.
3. Take heat off, then pour into mugs.
4. Enjoy a warm serving.

52.AUTUMN HARVEST

Time: 10 mins

Servings: 2

INGREDIENTS:

- 2 medium apples, cored and diced
- 1/2 cup of pumpkin puree
- 1 cup of almond milk

- 1 tbsp honey or maple syrup
- 1/2 tsp pumpkin pie spice
- Ice cubes

INSTRUCTIONS:

- Diced apples, pumpkin puree, almond milk, honey, maple syrup, pumpkin pie spice, and ice cubes Must all be put in a blender.
- Up to smooth, blend.
- Pour cold liquid into glasses and serve.

53.SPRING SPRITZER

Time: 5 mins

Servings: 1

INGREDIENTS:

- 1 cup of sparkling water
- 1/2 cup of fresh strawberries, split
- 1/2 cup of cucumber, split
- 1 tbsp fresh basil leaves, torn
- Juice of 1 lemon
- Ice cubes

INSTRUCTIONS:

1. Split strawberries, cucumber, torn basil leaves, sparkling water, lemon juice, and ice cubes Must all be placed in a glass.
2. Gently blend by stirring.
3. Enjoy while serving chilled.

54. HYDRATING HYDRATION

Time: 5 mins

Servings: 1

INGREDIENTS:

- 1 cup of coconut water
- 1/2 cup of watermelon chunks
- 1/2 cup of cucumber, split
- Juice of 1 lime
- 1 tbsp fresh mint leaves
- Ice cubes

INSTRUCTIONS:

1. Coconut water, watermelon chunks, cucumber slices, lime juice, fresh mint leaves, and ice cubes Must all be mixd in a blender.
2. Blend everything thoroughly.
3. Pour cold liquid into a glass and serve.

55. RASPBERRY RHAPSODY

Time: 5 mins

Servings: 1

INGREDIENTS:

- 1 cup of fresh raspberries
- 1/2 cup of Greek yogurt
- 1/2 cup of almond milk
- 1 tbsp honey or agave syrup
- Ice cubes

INSTRUCTIONS:

1. Blend fresh raspberries, Greek yogurt, almond milk, honey or agave syrup, and ice cubes together in a blender.
2. Up to smooth, blend.

3. Place in a glass and sip.

56MANGO MADNESS

Time: 5 mins

Servings: 1

INGREDIENTS:

- 1 cup of refrigerate mango chunks
- 1/2 cup of orange juice
- 1/2 cup of coconut water
- Juice of 1 lime
- 1 tbsp fresh mint leaves
- Ice cubes

INSTRUCTIONS:

1. Refrigerate mango chunks, ice cubes, orange juice, lime juice, coconut water, and fresh mint leaves Must all be blended together.
2. Blend everything thoroughly.
3. Pour cold liquid into a glass and serve.

57.PINEAPPLE PARADISE

Time: 5 mins

Servings: 1

INGREDIENTS:

- 1 cup of pineapple chunks
- 1/2 cup of coconut milk
- 1/2 cup of orange juice
- 1 tbsp shredded coconut
- Ice cubes

1. Pineapple chunks, coconut milk, orange juice, shredded coconut, and ice cubes Must all be blended together.
2. Up to smooth, blend.
3. Place in a glass and sip.

58.BERRY BLAST

Time: 5 mins

Servings: 1

INGREDIENTS:

- 1 cup of combined berries (strawberries, blueberries, raspberries)
- 1/2 cup of almond milk
- 1/2 cup of Greek yogurt
- 1 tbsp honey or agave syrup
- Ice cubes

INSTRUCTIONS:

1. Blend the combined berries, almond milk, Greek yogurt, honey or agave syrup, and ice cubes together in a blender.
2. Blend everything thoroughly.
3. Pour cold liquid into a glass and serve.

59.RADIANT GLOW

Time: 15 mins

Servings: 2

INGREDIENTS:

- 2 cups of spinach
- 1 cucumber
- 1 green apple
- 1 lemon
- 1-inch piece of ginger

- 1 cup of water

INSTRUCTIONS:

1. Thoroughly clean all the components.

2. Slice the ginger, cucumber, and green apple into mini pieces.

3. Lemon juice Must be squeezed.

4. Blend spinach, cucumber, green apple, ginger, lemon juice, and water together in a blender.

5. Up to smooth, blend.

6. Enjoy the brilliant radiance while serving chilled!

NUTRITION INFO (PER SERVING):

Cals: 80

Carbs: 20g

Protein: 2g

Fat: 0.5g

Fiber: 5g

60.SUPERFOOD SUPERSTAR

Time: 10 mins

Servings: 1

INGREDIENTS:

- 1 ripe banana
- 1 cup of combined berries (blueberries, raspberries, strawberries)
- 1 tbsp chia seeds
- 1 cup of almond milk
- 1 tbsp honey or maple syrup (non-compulsory)

INSTRUCTIONS:

1. Slice and peel the banana.

2. Banana, combined berries, chia seeds, almond milk, and sugar (if using) Must all be mixd in a blender.

3. Blend till creamy and smooth.

4. Pour this superfood superstar into a glass and savor it!

NUTRITION INFO (PER SERVING):

Cals: 280

Carbs: 55g

Protein: 5g

Fat: 7g

Fiber: 10g

61.GUT HEALTH GURU

Time: 20 mins

Servings: 4

INGREDIENTS:

- 2 cups of Greek yogurt
- 1 cup of combined berries (blueberries, raspberries, strawberries)
- 2 tbsp honey
- 1/4 cup of granola

INSTRUCTIONS:

1. Greek yogurt and honey are mixd in a bowl.

2. Mix thoroughly up to the honey is dispersed.

3. Layer the yogurt mixture, combined berries, and granola in serving glasses or bowls.

4. Till all the ingredients are utilized, keep adding layers.

5. Granola Must be sprinkled over top to finish.

6. Before serving, place in the fridge for at least 10 mins.

7. Enjoy this dessert recommended by a gastrointestinal expert!

NUTRITION INFO (PER SERVING):

Cals: 220

Carbs: 35g

Protein: 15g

Fat: 4g

Fiber: 4g

62.ALKALIZING ELIXIR

Time: 5 mins

Servings: 1

INGREDIENTS:

- 1 lemon
- 1 cucumber
- 1 tbsp fresh mint leaves
- 2 cups of water

INSTRUCTIONS:

1. Lemon juice Must be squeezed.

2. Make cucumber slices.

3. Lemon juice, cucumber slices, fresh mint leaves, and water Must all be mixd in a pitcher.

4. To let the flavors to meld, give it a good stir and a few mins to sit.

5. Enjoy the alkalizing elixir while serving chilled!

NUTRITION INFO (PER SERVING):

Cals: 10

Carbs: 3g

Protein: 0g

Fat: 0g

Fiber: 1g

63.SWEET AND TANGY

Time: 25 mins

Servings: 4

INGREDIENTS:

- 1 lb chicken breast, boneless and skinless
- 1/4 cup of honey
- 2 tbsp soy sauce
- 2 tbsp lemon juice
- 1 tbsp Dijon mustard
- 1 clove garlic, chop-up
- Salt and pepper as needed

INSTRUCTIONS:

1. Set the oven's temperature to 375°F (190°C).

2. Chicken breasts Must be salted and peppered.

3. Mix honey, soy sauce, lemon juice, Dijon mustard, and chop-up garlic in a mini bowl.

4. In a baking dish, put the chicken breasts and cover them with the honey mixture.

5. Bake for 20 mins, or up to the sauce has thickened and the chicken is thoroughly cooked.

6. Serve the acidic and sweet chicken with rice or steamed veggies.

NUTRITION INFO (PER SERVING):

Cals: 250

Carbs: 18g

Protein: 25g

Fat: 6g

Fiber: 0g

64. CREAMY DREAM

Time: 15 mins

Servings: 2

INGREDIENTS:

- 1 ripe avocado
- 1 banana
- 2 tbsp cocoa powder
- 1 cup of almond milk
- 1 tbsp honey or maple syrup (non-compulsory)
- 1/2 tsp vanilla extract

INSTRUCTIONS:

1. Take out the avocado's pit and scoop out the flesh after Cutting it in half.

2. Bananas Must be peel off and slice into pieces.

3. Avocado, banana, cocoa powder, almond milk, sweetener (if needed), and vanilla extract Must all be put in a blender.

4. Blend till creamy and smooth.

5. Pour this creamy dream into glasses and savor it!

NUTRITION INFO (PER SERVING):

Cals: 250

Carbs: 35g

Protein: 5g

Fat: 15g

Fiber: 10g

65.SPICY TWIST

Time: 30 mins

Servings: 4

INGREDIENTS:

- 1 lb shrimp, peel off and deveined
- 2 tbsp olive oil
- 2 cloves garlic, chop-up
- 1 tsp paprika
- 1/2 tsp cayenne pepper
- 1/2 tsp ground cumin
- Salt and pepper as needed
- Lime wedges, for serving

INSTRUCTIONS:

1. Olive oil, chop-up garlic, paprika, cumin, cayenne pepper, salt, and pepper are all mixd in a bowl.

2. To evenly coat the shrimp with the spice mixture, add them to the bowl and toss.

3. The shrimp are added to a heated skillet over medium-high heat.

4. The shrimp Must be cooked for two to three mins on every side, or up to pink and opaque throughout.

5. For an additional taste variation, serve the hot shrimp with wedges of lime.

NUTRITION INFO (PER SERVING):

Cals: 150

Carbs: 1g

Protein: 25g

Fat: 5g

Fiber: 0g

66.HERB INFUSION

Time: 10 mins

Servings: 2

INGREDIENTS:

- 2 cups of water
- 1 tbsp fresh herbs (such as mint, basil, or rosemary)

INSTRUCTIONS:

1. In a saucepan, bring the water to a boil.
2. To the boiling water, add the fresh herbs.
3. After 5 mins, turn off the heat and let the herbs steep.
4. Pour the infused liquid into mugs or cups of.
5. Take pleasure in the calming and fragrant herb infusion.

67. BRAIN BOOSTER

Time: 15 mins

Servings: 1

INGREDIENTS:

- 1 cup of combined berries (blueberries, strawberries, raspberries)
- 1/2 banana
- 1/2 cup of almond milk
- 1 tbsp almond butter
- 1 tbsp flaxseeds
- 1/2 tsp honey or maple syrup (non-compulsory)

INSTRUCTIONS:

1. Blend the combined berries, banana, flaxseeds, almond milk, almond butter, and sugar (if used) together in a blender.

2. Blend till creamy and smooth.

3. Pour the smoothie into a glass, then savor it!

NUTRITION INFO (PER SERVING):

Cals: 250

Carbs: 30g

Protein: 5g

Fat: 12g

Fiber: 8g

68. BONE STRENGTHENER

Time: 40 mins

Servings: 4

INGREDIENTS:

- 4 bone-in chicken thighs
- 2 tbsp olive oil
- 2 cloves garlic, chop-up
- 1 tsp dried rosemary
- 1 tsp dried thyme
- Salt and pepper as needed

INSTRUCTIONS:

1. Set the oven's temperature to 375°F (190°C).

2. Olive oil, chop-up garlic, dried thyme, dried rosemary, and salt & pepper are rubbed onto the chicken thighs.

3. The chicken thighs Must be put on a baking pan.

4. Bake the chicken for 30-35 mins, or up to the skin is crispy and the meat is thoroughly cooked.

5. With your preferred side dishes, serve the chicken thighs with bone strengthener.

NUTRITION INFO (PER SERVING):

Cals: 300

Carbs: 0g

Protein: 20g

Fat: 25g

Fiber: 0g

69.EYE HEALTH ELIXIR:

Time: 5 mins

Servings: 1

INGREDIENTS:

- 1 cup of carrot juice
- 1/2 cup of orange juice
- 1/4 cup of spinach
- 1/4 cup of blueberries

INSTRUCTIONS:

1. Blend the spinach, blueberries, orange juice, and carrot juice together in a blender.

2. Up to smooth, blend.

3. Pour into a glass, then sip.

NUTRITION INFO:

Cals: 120

Fat: 0g

Carbs: 28g

Protein: 2g

Vitamin A: 330% DV

Vitamin C: 150% DV

70. KID-FRIENDLY FAVORITE:

Time: 10 mins

Servings: 2

INGREDIENTS:

- 1 ripe banana
- 1 cup of strawberries, hulled
- 1/2 cup of plain Greek yogurt
- 1/2 cup of milk
- 1 tbsp honey (non-compulsory)

INSTRUCTIONS:

1. Banana, strawberries, Greek yogurt, milk, and honey (if used) Must all be mixd in a blender.

2. Blend till creamy and smooth.

3. Pour into glasses, then offer.

NUTRITION INFO:

Cals: 160

Fat: 2g

Carbs: 32g

Protein: 8g

Vitamin C: 90% DV

Calcium: 15% DV

71. LIQUID DESSERT:

Time: 5 mins

Servings: 1

INGREDIENTS:

- 1 cup of almond milk
- 1/2 cup of vanilla ice cream
- 2 tbsp chocolate syrup

INSTRUCTIONS:

1. Almond milk, vanilla ice cream, and chocolate syrup Must all be blended together.

2. Blend up to foamy and well mixd.

3. Pour into a glass, then sip.

NUTRITION INFO:

Cals: 300

Fat: 15g

Carbs: 36g

Protein: 6g

Calcium: 20% DV

72.BERRY BURST:

Time: 5 mins

Servings: 1

INGREDIENTS:

- 1 cup of combined berries (strawberries, blueberries, raspberries)
- 1/2 cup of cranberry juice
- 1/2 cup of yogurt (any flavor)

INSTRUCTIONS:

1. The combined berries, cranberry juice, and yogurt Must all be mixd in a blender.

2. Up to smooth, blend.

3. Pour into a glass, then sip.

NUTRITION INFO:

Cals: 150

Fat: 1g

Carbs: 32g

Protein: 5g

Vitamin C: 100% DV

73.GREEN MACHINE:

Time: 5 mins

Servings: 1

INGREDIENTS:

- 1 cup of spinach
- 1/2 cup of cucumber, chop-up
- 1/2 cup of green grapes
- 1/2 cup of pineapple chunks
- 1/2 cup of coconut water

INSTRUCTIONS:

1. Blend the spinach, cucumber, green grapes, pineapple pieces, and coconut water together in a blender.

2. Up to smooth, blend.

3. Pour into a glass, then sip.

NUTRITION INFO:

Cals: 100

Fat: 1g

Carbs: 25g

Protein: 2g

Vitamin A: 50% DV

Vitamin C: 70% DV

74.CITRUS SENSATION:

Time: 5 mins

Servings: 1

INGREDIENTS:

- 1 orange, peel off
- 1/2 grapefruit, peel off
- 1/2 lemon, peel off
- 1/2 lime, peel off
- 1 tbsp honey (non-compulsory)

INSTRUCTIONS:

1. Orange, grapefruit, lemon, lime, and honey (if preferred) Must all be mixd in a blender.

2. Up to smooth, blend.

3. Pour into a glass, then sip.

NUTRITION INFO:

Cals: 80

Fat: 0g

Carbs: 21g

Protein: 1g

Vitamin C: 120% DV

75. VEGGIE DELIGHT:

Time: 10 mins

Servings: 2

INGREDIENTS:

- 1 cup of kale
- 1/2 cucumber, chop-up
- 1/2 bell pepper, chop-up
- 1/2 carrot, chop-up
- 1/4 cup of parsley
- 1 cup of coconut water

INSTRUCTIONS:

1. Kale, cucumber, bell pepper, carrot, parsley, and coconut water Must all be mixd in a blender.

2. Up to smooth, blend.

3. Pour into glasses, then offer.

NUTRITION INFO:

Cals: 70

Fat: 0g

Carbs: 16g

Protein: 3g

Vitamin A: 180% DV

Vitamin C: 80% DV

76. POWER PUNCH:

Time: 5 mins

Servings: 1

INGREDIENTS:

- 1 cup of pineapple juice
- 1/2 cup of mango, chop-up
- 1/2 cup of strawberries, hulled
- 1 tbsp chia seeds

INSTRUCTIONS:

1. Mango, strawberries, pineapple juice, and chia seeds Must all be mixd in a blender.

2. Blend everything thoroughly.

3. Pour into a glass, then sip.

NUTRITION INFO:

Cals: 160

Fat: 2g

Carbs: 38g

Protein: 3g

Vitamin C: 150% DV

Fiber: 7g

77.RAINBOW REFRESHER:

Time: 5 mins

Servings: 1

INGREDIENTS:

- 1/2 cup of pineapple chunks
- 1/2 cup of mango, chop-up
- 1/2 cup of papaya, chop-up
- 1/2 cup of coconut water

INSTRUCTIONS:

1. Blend the pineapple chunks, mango, papaya, and coconut water together in a blender.

2. Up to smooth, blend.

3. Pour into a glass, then sip.

NUTRITION INFO:

Cals: 120

Fat: 1g

Carbs: 30g

Protein: 2g

Vitamin C: 150% DV

78. ENERGIZING GREEN:

Time: 5 mins

Servings: 1

INGREDIENTS:

- 1 cup of spinach
- 1/2 cup of green apple, chop-up
- 1/2 cup of cucumber, chop-up
- 1/2 cup of celery, chop-up
- 1/2 cup of coconut water

INSTRUCTIONS:

1. Blend the spinach, green apple, cucumber, celery, and coconut water together in a blender.

2. Up to smooth, blend.

3. Pour into a glass, then sip.

NUTRITION INFO:

Cals: 80

Fat: 0g

Carbs: 20g

Protein: 2g

Vitamin A: 100% DV

Vitamin C: 50% DV

79. ZESTY LEMONADE:

Time: 10 mins

Servings: 4

INGREDIENTS:

- 4 lemons
- 4 cups of water
- 1/2 cup of sugar
- Ice cubes

INSTRUCTIONS:

1. Lemon juice Must be squeezed, then the seeds Must be strained out.
2. Mix the lemon juice, water, and sugar in a pitcher. Stir the sugar up to it melts.
3. Re-stir the pitcher after adding the ice cubes.
4. Cool the tangy lemonade before serving.

80. ORANGE CRUSH:

Time: 5 mins

Servings: 1

INGREDIENTS:

- 1 Big orange
- 1/2 cup of sparkling water
- Ice cubes

INSTRUCTIONS:

1. Orange juice Must be squeezed, and pulp Must be strained out.
2. Mix orange juice and sparkling water in a glass.
3. Ice cubes Must be added to the glass. Gently swirl.
4. Enjoy your orange crush, it's refreshing.

81. CARROT CAKE:

Time: 1 hr 30 mins

Servings: 12

INGREDIENTS:

- 2 cups of all-purpose flour
- 2 cups of finely grated carrots
- 1 cup of sugar
- 1/2 cup of vegetable oil
- 1/2 cup of unsweetened applesauce
- 3 eggs
- 1 tsp baking powder
- 1 tsp baking soda
- 1/2 tsp salt
- 1/2 tsp cinnamon
- 1/4 tsp nutmeg
- Cream cheese frosting (store-bought or homemade)

INSTRUCTIONS:

1. Grease a 9x13-inch baking pan and preheat the oven to 350°F (175°C).
2. Mix the flour, sugar, baking soda, salt, cinnamon, and nutmeg in a big bowl.
3. Mix the vegetable oil, applesauce, and eggs in a another bowl. Stir in the carrots that have been shredded.
4. Mix the dry ingredients briefly while you add the liquid ingredients one at a time.
5. Smooth the top after pouring the mixture into the prepared baking pan.
6. A toothpick placed in the center of the cake Must come out clean after 35 to 40 mins of baking.
7. The carrot cake Must be completely cooled before cream cheese icing is applied.
8. Serve after Cutting into slices.

82. BEETROOT BOOST:

Time: 15 mins

Servings: 2

INGREDIENTS:

- 2 medium-sized beetroots
- 2 Big carrots
- 1 apple
- 1-inch piece of ginger
- 1 tbsp lemon juice
- Honey or maple syrup (non-compulsory, for sweetness)
- Ice cubes

INSTRUCTIONS:

1. Apple, ginger, beets, and carrots Must all be peel off and chop-up.
2. Lemon juice, a little water, and the chop-up ingredients Must all be put in a blender.
3. Blend till creamy and smooth. Add honey or maple syrup for sweetness if preferred.
4. Beetroot boost Must be poured into ice-filled glasses.
5. Stir, then savor the flavorful, healthy beverage.

83. PINEAPPLE PARADISE:

Time: 5 mins

Servings: 1

INGREDIENTS:

- 1 cup of pineapple chunks
- 1/2 cup of coconut milk
- 1/4 cup of orange juice
- Ice cubes

INSTRUCTIONS:

1. Orange juice, coconut milk, and pineapple chunks Must all be blended together.
2. Blend till creamy and smooth.

3. Into an ice-filled glass, pour the pineapple paradise.
4. Serve the tropical flavors and enjoy them.

84.MANGO TANGO:

Time: 10 mins

Servings: 2

INGREDIENTS:

- 2 ripe mangoes
- 1 cup of plain yogurt
- 1/2 cup of orange juice
- 1 tbsp honey
- Ice cubes

INSTRUCTIONS:

1. Mangoes Must be peel off and chop-up without the pit.
2. The split mangoes, plain yogurt, orange juice, and honey Must all be blended together.
3. Blend till creamy and smooth.
4. Pour the mango tango over ice-filled glasses.
5. Stir, then savor the wonderful mango tastes.

85.WATERMELON WAVE:

Time: 10 mins

Servings: 4

INGREDIENTS:

- 4 cups of diced watermelon
- 1 tbsp lime juice
- 1 tbsp honey
- Fresh mint leaves for garnish
- Ice cubes

INSTRUCTIONS:

1. Watermelon dice, lime juice, and honey Must all be mixd in a blender.
2. Up to smooth, blend.
3. Pour the watermelon wave over ice-filled glasses.
4. Use fresh mint leaves as a garnish.
5. Drink up and savor the delicious watermelon flavor.

86.MINT MOJITO:

Time: 5 mins

Servings: 1

INGREDIENTS:

- 6-8 fresh mint leaves
- 1 lime
- 2 tbsp sugar
- 1/2 cup of sparkling water
- Ice cubes

INSTRUCTIONS:

1. Mint leaves, sugar, and lime juice are mushed together in a glass.
2. To the glass, add ice cubes.
3. Add sparkling water on top, then gently swirl.
4. Add a lime slice and a mint sprig as garnish.
5. Enjoy a cool mojito with mint.

87.KALEIDOSCOPE:

Time: 10 mins

Servings: 2

INGREDIENTS:

- 2 cups of kale leaves
- 1 cup of cucumber slices
- 1/2 cup of pineapple chunks
- 1/2 cup of green grapes
- 1 tbsp lemon juice
- 1 cup of coconut water
- Ice cubes

INSTRUCTIONS:

1. In a glass, lime juice, sugar, and mint leaves are all mixd.
2. Add ice cubes to the glass.
3. On top, pour sparkling water and give it a gentle stir.
4. As a garnish, include a lime slice and a mint leaf.
5. Enjoy a refreshing mint-based mojito.

88.GINGER ALE

Time: 5 mins

Servings: 1

INGREDIENTS:

- 1 cup of ginger ale
- 1/2 lime, juiced
- Ice cubes
- Fresh mint leaves, for garnish

INSTRUCTIONS:

1. Ice cubes Must be added to a glass.

2. Fill the glass with ginger ale.

3. Half a lime's juice Must be squeezed into the glass.

4. Gently blend by stirring.

5. Use fresh mint leaves as a garnish.

6. Dispense and savor!

NUTRITION INFO (PER SERVING):

Cals: 110

Carbs: 28g

Fat: 0g

Protein: 0g

Fiber: 0g

89.POMEGRANATE PERFECTION

Time: 10 mins

Servings: 2

INGREDIENTS:

- 1 cup of pomegranate juice
- 1/2 cup of orange juice
- 1/4 cup of lime juice
- 1 tbsp honey
- Ice cubes
- Pomegranate arils, for garnish

INSTRUCTIONS:

1. Pomegranate juice, orange juice, lime juice, and honey Must all be mixd in a pitcher.

2. Stir up to honey is well mixd and dissolved.

3. Add ice cubes to the cups of.

4. Over the ice, pour the pomegranate mixture.

5. Add pomegranate arils as a garnish.

6. Dispense and savor!

NUTRITION INFO (PER SERVING):

Cals: 110

Carbs: 28g

Fat: 0g

Protein: 1g

Fiber: 0g

90.BLUE VELVET

Time: 1 hr

Servings: 12

INGREDIENTS:

- 2 1/2 cups of all-purpose flour
- 1 1/2 cups of granulated sugar
- 1 tsp baking soda
- 1 tsp salt
- 2 tbsp unsweetened cocoa powder
- 1 1/2 cups of vegetable oil
- 1 cup of buttermilk

- 2 Big eggs
- 2 tbsp blue food coloring
- 1 tsp white vinegar
- 1 tsp vanilla extract

INSTRUCTIONS:

1. Oven Must be heated to 350°F (175°C). Prepare two 9-inch round cake pans with oil and flour.

2. Mix the flour, sugar, baking soda, salt, and cocoa powder in a sizable bowl.

3. Mix vegetable oil, buttermilk, eggs, food coloring, vinegar, and vanilla essence in a separate basin.

4. Mix thoroughly after gradually incorporating the wet components into the dry ones.

5. Between the prepared cake pans, distribute the batter equally.

6. 30 to 35 mins of baking time, or up to a toothpick inserted in the center of the cake comes out clean.

7. After taking the cakes out of the oven, let them cool in the pans for ten mins. Afterward, transfer to a wire rack to entirely cool.

8. Cakes can be frosted with cream cheese icing or any other frosting of choice.

9. Slice, then dish.

NUTRITION INFO (PER SERVING):

Cals: 410

Carbs: 47g

Fat: 23g

Protein: 4g

Fiber: 1g

91.RASPBERRY RIPPLE

Time: 15 mins

Servings: 4

INGREDIENTS:

- 2 cups of vanilla ice cream
- 1 cup of fresh or refrigerate raspberries
- 2 tbsp powdered sugar
- 1 tsp vanilla extract
- Fresh mint leaves, for garnish

INSTRUCTIONS:

1. Blend vanilla ice cream, raspberries, sugar, and vanilla essence together in a blender.

2. Blend till creamy and smooth.

3. Place serving glasses with the raspberry mixture inside.

4. Create a ripple effect by gently swirling around the mixture with a spoon or skewer.

5. Use fresh mint leaves as a garnish.

6. Serve right away and delight in!

NUTRITION INFO (PER SERVING):

Cals: 220

Carbs: 30g

Fat: 10g

Protein: 3g

Fiber: 4g

92.CREAMSICLE DREAM

Time: 5 mins

Servings: 1

INGREDIENTS:

- 1 cup of orange juice
- 1/2 cup of vanilla ice cream
- 1/4 cup of milk
- 1 tbsp honey
- Ice cubes

INSTRUCTIONS:

1. Orange juice, vanilla ice cream, milk, and honey Must all be blended together.

2. Blend till creamy and smooth.

3. When completely mixd, add the ice cubes and blend one more.

4. Put some in a glass.

5. Dispense and savor!

NUTRITION INFO (PER SERVING):

Cals: 230

Carbs: 49g

Fat: 3g

Protein: 3g

Fiber: 1g

93.KIWI KISS

Time: 10 mins

Servings: 2

INGREDIENTS:

- 2 ripe kiwis, peel off and split
- 1 cup of pineapple juice
- 1/2 cup of coconut milk
- 1 tbsp honey
- Ice cubes
- Kiwi slices, for garnish

INSTRUCTIONS:

1. Kiwi slices, pineapple juice, coconut milk, and honey Must all be mixd in a blender.

2. Up to smooth, blend.

3. When completely mixd, add the ice cubes and blend one more.

4. Add liquid to glasses.

5. Slices of kiwi are a garnish.

6. Dispense and savor!

NUTRITION INFO (PER SERVING):

Cals: 180

Carbs: 34g

Fat: 4g

Protein: 2g

Fiber: 4g

94.PEAR PLEASURE

Time: 10 mins

Servings: 2

INGREDIENTS:

- 2 ripe pears, peel off and chop-up
- 1 cup of apple juice
- 1/2 cup of plain yogurt
- 1 tbsp honey
- Ice cubes
- Fresh mint leaves, for garnish

INSTRUCTIONS:

1. Chop-up pears, apple juice, yogurt, and honey Must all be mixd in a blender.

2. Blend till creamy and smooth.

3. When completely mixd, add the ice cubes and blend one more.

4. Add liquid to glasses.

5. Use fresh mint leaves as a garnish.

6. Dispense and savor!

NUTRITION INFO (PER SERVING):

Cals: 180

Carbs: 40g

Fat: 2g

Protein: 3g

Fiber: 6g

95.PEVERY PARADISE

Time: 10 mins

Servings: 2

INGREDIENTS:

- 2 ripe peveryes, peel off and pitted
- 1 cup of orange juice
- 1/2 cup of coconut water
- 1 tbsp lemon juice
- Ice cubes
- Fresh mint leaves, for garnish

INSTRUCTIONS:

1. Peveryes, orange juice, coconut water, and lemon juice are all mixd in a blender.

2. Blend till creamy and smooth.

3. When completely mixd, add the ice cubes and blend one more.

4. Add liquid to glasses.

5. Use fresh mint leaves as a garnish.

6. Dispense and savor!

NUTRITION INFO (PER SERVING):

Cals: 120

Carbs: 28g

Fat: 1g

Protein: 3g

Fiber: 3g

96. STRAWBERRY SWIRL

Time: 10 mins

Servings: 2

INGREDIENTS:

- 1 1/2 cups of fresh strawberries, hulled
- 1 cup of milk
- 1/2 cup of vanilla yogurt
- 1 tbsp honey
- Ice cubes
- Fresh strawberries, split, for garnish

INSTRUCTIONS:

1. Blend milk, yogurt, honey, and fresh strawberries in a blender.

2. Blend till creamy and smooth.

3. When completely mixd, add the ice cubes and blend one more.

4. Add liquid to glasses.

5. Slice some fresh strawberries to garnish.

6. Dispense and savor!

NUTRITION INFO (PER SERVING):

Cals: 150

Carbs: 27g

Fat: 2g

Protein: 7g

Fiber: 3g

97. MELON MADNESS

Time: 10 mins

Servings: 2

INGREDIENTS:

- 2 cups of diced combined melons (watermelon, cantaloupe, honeydew)
- 1/2 cup of pineapple juice
- 1/4 cup of lime juice
- 1 tbsp agave syrup or honey
- Ice cubes
- Fresh mint leaves, for garnish

INSTRUCTIONS:

1. Diced combined melon, pineapple juice, lime juice, and agave syrup Must all be mixd in a blender.

2. Blend everything thoroughly up to it's smooth.

3. As needed, add ice cubes and mix once more.

4. Add liquid to glasses.

5. Use fresh mint leaves as a garnish.

6. Dispense and savor!

NUTRITION INFO (PER SERVING):

Cals: 90

Carbs: 23g

Fat: 0g

Protein: 1g

Fiber: 2g

98. GOLDEN SUNSHINE

Time: 10 mins

Servings: 2

INGREDIENTS:

- 2 oranges, peel off
- 1 carrot, peel off and chop-up
- 1-inch piece of ginger, peel off

INSTRUCTIONS:

1. Oranges, carrots, and ginger Must be added to a juicer.
2. The components Must be blended and smooth after processing.
3. Juice Must be poured into glasses and served right away.

99. RECIPE: MINTY FRESH

Time: 5 mins

Servings: 1

INGREDIENTS:

- 1 cucumber, peel off and chop-up
- 1 cup of fresh mint leaves
- 1 lemon, juiced
- 1 tsp honey (non-compulsory)

INSTRUCTIONS:

1. Cucumber, mint leaves, lemon juice, and honey (if preferred) Must all be mixd in a blender.
2. Blend everything thoroughly up to it's smooth.
3. Place the cold mixture in a glass and serve.

100.RECIPE: GREEN REVIVAL

Time: 8 mins

Servings: 1

INGREDIENTS:

- 1 green apple, cored and chop-up
- 1 cup of spinach leaves
- 1/2 cucumber, peel off and chop-up
- 1/2 lime, juiced

INSTRUCTIONS:

1. To a blender, add the green apple, spinach leaves, cucumber, and lime juice.
2. Blend till creamy and smooth.
3. Enjoy the combination after pouring it into a glass.

101.BERRY BONANZA

Time: 5 mins

Servings: 2

INGREDIENTS:

- 1 cup of combined berries (strawberries, blueberries, raspberries)
- 1 banana, peel off and split
- 1 cup of almond milk (or any preferred milk)
- 1 tbsp honey (non-compulsory)

INSTRUCTIONS:

1. In a blender, mix the combined berries, banana, almond milk, and honey (if using).
2. Blend everything thoroughly up to it's smooth.
3. Place cold drinks in glasses after pouring the mixture.

102. CITRUS SYMPHONY

Time: 7 mins

Servings: 2

INGREDIENTS:

- 2 oranges, peel off
- 1 grapefruit, peel off
- 2 limes, juiced
- 1 tbsp agave syrup (non-compulsory)

INSTRUCTIONS:

1. Utilize an orange and grapefruit juicer to extract the juice.
2. Mix the lime juice and agave syrup (if using) in a separate bowl.
3. Citrus liquids Must be poured into glasses before the lime mixture is drizzled on top.
4. Stir thoroughly, then serve cold.

103. VEGGIE VITALITY

Time: 10 mins

Servings: 2

INGREDIENTS:

- 2 carrots, peel off and chop-up
- 2 tomatoes, chop-up
- 1 celery stalk, chop-up
- 1/2 cucumber, peel off and chop-up
- 1/2 bell pepper, seeded and chop-up
- 1/2 lemon, juiced

INSTRUCTIONS:

1. Use a blender or juicer to mix all the ingredients.
2. Process up to incorporated and well-mixd.
3. Juice Must be poured into glasses and served right away.

104. POWER POTION

Time: 6 mins

Servings: 1

INGREDIENTS:

- 1 cup of pineapple chunks
- 1/2 cup of coconut water
- 1 tbsp chia seeds
- 1 tsp spirulina powder (non-compulsory)

INSTRUCTIONS:

1. The pineapple chunks, coconut water, chia seeds, and spirulina powder (if used) Must all be mixd in a blender.
2. Blend up to well-mixd and smooth.
3. Enjoy the potion after pouring it into a glass.

105. RAINBOW RIOT

Time: 5 mins

Servings: 1

INGREDIENTS:

- 1 mini beet, peel off and chop-up
- 1 carrot, peel off and chop-up
- 1/2 orange, peel off
- 1/2 lemon, juiced
- 1 cup of coconut water

INSTRUCTIONS:

1. To a blender, add the beet, carrot, orange, lemon juice, and coconut water.
2. Blend till glossy and colorful.
3. Place the cold mixture in a glass and serve.

106. LEMON LIME FUSION

Time: 5 mins

Servings: 1

INGREDIENTS:

- 2 lemons, juiced
- 2 limes, juiced
- 1 cup of sparkling water
- 1 tbsp honey (non-compulsory)

INSTRUCTIONS:

1. Mix the lemon juice, lime juice, sparkling water, and honey (if using) in a pitcher.
2. Up to the honey is dissolved, stir thoroughly.
3. Place ice in a glass with the fusion and serve.

107. ORANGE OASIS

Time: 5 mins

Servings: 1

INGREDIENTS:

- 2 oranges, peel off
- 1/2 cup of coconut milk
- 1 tbsp agave syrup (non-compulsory)
- Ice cubes

INSTRUCTIONS:

1. Use a citrus juicer to extract the orange juice.
2. Orange juice, coconut milk, ice cubes, and agave syrup (if used) Must all be blended together.
3. Blend up to frothed up and creamy.
4. Place the oasis in a glass, then sip.

108.CARROT CRAZE:

Time: 5 mins

Servings: 2

INGREDIENTS:

- 2 carrots, chop-up
- 1 banana
- 1 cup of orange juice
- 1/2 cup of Greek yogurt
- 1 tbsp honey

INSTRUCTIONS:

1. Blend the items together in a blender.
2. Blend till creamy and smooth.
3. Pour into glasses, then offer.

109.BEETROOT BLISS:

Time: 7 mins

Servings: 2

INGREDIENTS:

- 1 mini beetroot, peel off and chop-up
- 1 cup of refrigerate combined berries
- 1 cup of almond milk
- 1 tbsp chia seeds
- 1 tbsp honey

INSTRUCTIONS:

1. To a blender, add all the ingredients.
2. Blend everything thoroughly and smoothly.
3. Fill glasses with liquid and sip.

110. PINEAPPLE PARTY:

Time: 5 mins

Servings: 2

INGREDIENTS:

- 1 cup of fresh pineapple chunks
- 1 banana
- 1/2 cup of coconut milk
- 1/2 cup of plain yogurt
- .1 tbsp lime juice

INSTRUCTIONS:

1. In a blender, mix all the ingredients.
2. Blend till creamy and smooth.
3. Pour cold liquid into glasses and serve.

111. MANGO MAGIC:

Time: 5 mins

Servings: 2

INGREDIENTS:

- 1 ripe mango, peel off and diced
- 1 banana
- 1/2 cup of orange juice
- 1/2 cup of Greek yogurt
- 1 tbsp honey

INSTRUCTIONS:

1. Blend the items together in a blender.
2. Blend till creamy and smooth.
3. Fill glasses with liquid and sip.

112. WATERMELON WHIRL:

Time: 5 mins

Servings: 2

INGREDIENTS:

- 2 cups of fresh watermelon, diced
- 1 cup of refrigerate strawberries
- 1/2 cup of coconut water
- 1 tbsp lime juice
- 1 tsp agave nectar (non-compulsory)

INSTRUCTIONS:

1. To a blender, add all the ingredients.
2. Blend everything thoroughly up to it's smooth.
3. Pour cold liquid into glasses and serve.

113. GINGER SPICE:

Time: 5 mins

Servings: 2

INGREDIENTS:

- 1 cup of pineapple chunks
- 1 mini apple, peel off and chop-up
- 1 mini piece of fresh ginger, peel off
- 1 cup of almond milk
- 1 tbsp honey

INSTRUCTIONS:

1. Blend the items together in a blender.
2. Blend till creamy and smooth.
3. Fill glasses with liquid and sip.

114. POMEGRANATE POTION:

Time: 5 mins

Servings: 2

INGREDIENTS:

- 1 cup of pomegranate seeds
- 1 banana
- 1/2 cup of coconut water
- 1/2 cup of Greek yogurt
- 1 tbsp honey

INSTRUCTIONS:

1. In a blender, mix all the ingredients.
2. Blend up to well-mixd and smooth.
3. Pour cold liquid into glasses and serve.

115. BLUEBERRY BURST:

Time: 5 mins

Servings: 2

INGREDIENTS:

- 1 cup of refrigerate blueberries
- 1 banana
- 1 cup of almond milk
- 1 tbsp honey
- 1/2 tsp vanilla extract

INSTRUCTIONS:

1. To a blender, add all the ingredients.
2. Blend till creamy and smooth.
3. Fill glasses with liquid and sip.

116.RASPBERRY RHAPSODY:

Time: 5 mins

Servings: 2

INGREDIENTS:

- 1 cup of refrigerate raspberries
- 1/2 cup of plain yogurt
- 1/2 cup of almond milk
- 1 tbsp honey
- 1/2 tsp lemon zest

INSTRUCTIONS:

1. Blend the items together in a blender.
2. Blend everything thoroughly up to it's smooth.
3. Pour cold liquid into glasses and serve.

117.CREAMY CITRUS:

Time: 5 mins

Servings: 2

INGREDIENTS:

- 1 orange, peel off and segmented
- 1 banana
- 1/2 cup of coconut milk
- 1/2 cup of Greek yogurt
- 1 tbsp honey

INSTRUCTIONS:

1. In a blender, mix all the ingredients.
2. Blend till creamy and smooth.
3. Fill glasses with liquid and sip.

118.KIWI DELIGHT:

Time: 10 mins

Servings: 2

INGREDIENTS:

- 2 ripe kiwis
- 1 cup of Greek yogurt
- 1 tbsp honey
- 1/2 cup of crushed ice

INSTRUCTIONS:

1. Kiwis Must be peel off and split into mini pieces.
2. The kiwis, Greek yogurt, honey, and ice cubes Must all be mixd in a blender.
3. Blend till creamy and smooth.
4. Pour cold liquid into glasses and serve.

NUTRITION INFO (PER SERVING):

Cals: 150

Protein: 10g

Carbs: 28g

Fat: 1g

Fiber: 3g

119.PEAR PARADISE:

Time: 15 mins

Servings: 4

INGREDIENTS:

- 2 ripe pears, peel off and cored
- 1 cup of spinach leaves
- 1 banana
- 1/2 cup of almond milk
- 1 tbsp chia seeds
- 1/2 tsp vanilla extract

INSTRUCTIONS:

1. Make mini slices in the pears.

2. The diced pears, spinach, banana, almond milk, chia seeds, and vanilla essence Must all be mixd in a blender.

3. Blend till creamy and smooth.

4. Pour cold liquid into glasses and serve.

NUTRITION INFO (PER SERVING):

Cals: 120

Protein: 3g

Carbs: 24g

Fat: 2g

Fiber: 7g

120.PEVERY PERFECTION:

Time: 12 mins

Servings: 3

INGREDIENTS:

- 2 ripe peveryes, pitted and split
- 1 cup of unsweetened coconut milk
- 1/2 cup of orange juice
- 1 tbsp honey
- 1/2 tsp finely grated ginger

INSTRUCTIONS:

1. Peveryes, coconut milk, orange juice, honey, and ginger that has been finely grated are all mixd in a blender.

2. Blend till creamy and smooth.

3. Pour cold liquid into glasses and serve.

NUTRITION INFO (PER SERVING):

Cals: 110

Protein: 1g

Carbs: 24g

Fat: 3g

Fiber: 2g

121.STRAWBERRY SMOOTHIE:

Time: 8 mins

Servings: 2

INGREDIENTS:

- 1 cup of strawberries
- 1 banana
- 1 cup of almond milk
- 1 tbsp honey
- 1/2 cup of crushed ice

INSTRUCTIONS:

1. Strawberries, banana, almond milk, honey, and ice cubes Must all be mixd in a blender.

2. Blend till creamy and smooth.

3. Pour cold liquid into glasses and serve.

NUTRITION INFO (PER SERVING):

Cals: 120

Protein: 2g

Carbs: 27g

Fat: 2g

Fiber: 4g

122.MELON MANIA:

Time: 10 mins

Servings: 2

INGREDIENTS:

- 1 cup of cubed watermelon
- 1 cup of cubed cantaloupe
- 1 cup of cubed honeydew melon
- 1/2 cup of coconut water
- Juice of 1 lime
- Fresh mint leaves (for garnish)

INSTRUCTIONS:

1. Blend the watermelon, cantaloupe, honeydew melon, coconut water, and lime juice together in a blender.

2. Blend everything thoroughly up to it's smooth.

3. Serve chilled after pouring into glasses and adding fresh mint leaves as a garnish.

NUTRITION INFO (PER SERVING):

Cals: 80

Protein: 1g

Carbs: 19g

Fat: 0g

Fiber: 2g

123.GOLDEN ELIXIR:

Time: 5 mins

Servings: 1

INGREDIENTS:

- 1 cup of fresh orange juice
- 1/2 tsp turmeric powder
- 1/4 tsp ginger powder
- 1 tbsp honey

INSTRUCTIONS:

1. Juice from a fresh orange, turmeric, ginger, and honey Must all be mixd in a glass.

2. Stir everything up thoroughly up to well-mixd.

3. Serve right away.

NUTRITION INFO (PER SERVING):

Cals: 120

Protein: 1g

Carbs: 28g

Fat: 0g

Fiber: 0g

124.MINT MARVEL:

Time: 7 mins

Servings: 1

INGREDIENTS:

- 1 cup of fresh pineapple chunks
- 1/2 cup of coconut water
- 1/4 cup of fresh mint leaves
- 1 tbsp lime juice
- 1/2 tsp honey

INSTRUCTIONS:

1. The pineapple chunks, coconut water, mint leaves, lime juice, and honey Must all be blended together.

2. Blend everything thoroughly up to it's smooth.

3. Pour cold liquid into a glass and serve.

NUTRITION INFO (PER SERVING):

Cals: 90

Protein: 1g

Carbs: 22g

Fat: 0g

Fiber: 2g

125.GREEN GARDEN:

Time: 10 mins

Servings: 2

INGREDIENTS:

- 2 cups of spinach leaves
- 1 ripe banana
- 1/2 cup of chop-up cucumber
- 1/2 cup of chop-up green apple
- 1/2 cup of almond milk
- 1 tbsp chia seeds

INSTRUCTIONS:

1. Blend the spinach leaves, banana, cucumber, green apple, chia seeds, and almond milk in a food processor.

2. Blend till creamy and smooth.

3. Pour cold liquid into glasses and serve.

NUTRITION INFO (PER SERVING):

Cals: 120

Protein: 3g

Carbs: 24g

Fat: 2g

Fiber: 7g

126. BERRY BOOST:

Time: 8 mins

Servings: 2

INGREDIENTS:

- 1 cup of combined berries (strawberries, blueberries, raspberries)
- 1 ripe banana
- 1 cup of almond milk
- 1 tbsp honey
- 1/2 cup of crushed ice

INSTRUCTIONS:

1. The combined berries, banana, almond milk, honey, and crushed ice Must all be mixd in a blender.
2. Blend till creamy and smooth.
3. Pour cold liquid into glasses and serve.

NUTRITION INFO (PER SERVING):

Cals: 130

Protein: 2g

Carbs: 29g

Fat: 2g

Fiber: 6g

127. CITRUS DELIGHT:

Time: 7 mins

Servings: 2

INGREDIENTS:

- 1 grapefruit, peel off and segmented
- 2 oranges, peel off and segmented
- 1 lemon, juiced
- 1 tbsp honey
- Fresh mint leaves (for garnish)

INSTRUCTIONS:

1. Blend the grapefruit, orange, and lemon juices with the honey in a blender.

2. Blend everything thoroughly.

3. Serve chilled after pouring into glasses and adding fresh mint leaves as a garnish.

NUTRITION INFO (PER SERVING):

Cals: 90

Protein: 2g

Carbs: 22g

Fat: 0g

Fiber: 4g

128.VEGGIE HEAVEN:

Time: 10 mins

Servings: 2

INGREDIENTS:

- 2 cups of spinach leaves
- 1 cucumber, peel off and chop-up
- 2 celery stalks, chop-up
- 1 green apple, cored and chop-up
- 1 lemon, juiced
- 1-inch piece of ginger, peel off
- 1 cup of water

INSTRUCTIONS:

1. Blend the items together in a blender.

2. Blend everything thoroughly up to it's smooth.

3. To get rid of any pulp, strain the mixture if required.

4. Pour cold liquid into glasses and serve.

NUTRITION INFO (PER SERVING):

Cals: 80

Carbs: 20g

Protein: 2g

Fat: 0.5g

Fiber: 5g

129. POWER BLEND:

Time: 5 mins

Servings: 1

INGREDIENTS:

- 1 banana
- 1 cup of spinach leaves
- 1 cup of almond milk
- 1 tbsp chia seeds
- 1 tbsp honey or maple syrup (non-compulsory)
- Ice cubes (non-compulsory)

INSTRUCTIONS:

1. Blend the items together in a blender.

2. Blend till creamy and smooth.

3. If desired, add ice cubes and mix one more.

4. Place in a glass and sip.

NUTRITION INFO (PER SERVING):

Cals: 250

Carbs: 45g

Protein: 8g

Fat: 6g

Fiber: 10g

130.RAINBOW SPLASH:

Time: 5 mins

Servings: 1

INGREDIENTS:

- 1 cup of combined berries (strawberries, blueberries, raspberries)
- 1 cup of coconut water
- 1 tbsp lime juice
- 1 tbsp honey or agave syrup (non-compulsory)
- Ice cubes

INSTRUCTIONS:

1. Blend the items together in a blender.

2. Blend everything thoroughly up to it's smooth.

3. When the appropriate consistency is attained, add ice cubes and mix once more.

4. Pour cold liquid into a glass and serve.

NUTRITION INFO (PER SERVING):

Cals: 120

Carbs: 30g

Protein: 2g

Fat: 0.5g

Fiber: 6g

131.LEMONADE TWIST:

Time: 10 mins

Servings: 4

INGREDIENTS:

- 4 lemons, juiced
- 4 cups of water
- 4 tbsp honey or sugar (adjust as needed)
- Fresh mint leaves for garnish (non-compulsory)
- Split lemon for garnish (non-compulsory)
- Ice cubes

INSTRUCTIONS:

1. Mix lemon juice, water, and sweetener in a pitcher.

2. Once the sweetener has dissolved, thoroughly stir.

3. Re-stir, then add the ice cubes.

4. If preferred, garnish with lemon slices and fresh mint leaves.

5. Offer cold.

NUTRITION INFO (PER SERVING):

Cals: 30

Carbs: 10g

Protein: 0g

Fat: 0g

Fiber: 0g

132.ORANGE DELIGHT:

Time: 5 mins

Servings: 2

INGREDIENTS:

- 2 Big oranges, peel off and segmented
- 1 cup of almond milk
- 1 tbsp honey or maple syrup (non-compulsory)
- Ice cubes

INSTRUCTIONS:

1. Oranges, almond milk, and sugar (if using) Must all be added to a blender.

2. Blend till creamy and smooth.

3. When the appropriate consistency is attained, add ice cubes and mix once more.

4. Pour cold liquid into glasses and serve.

NUTRITION INFO (PER SERVING):

Cals: 100

Carbs: 20g

Protein: 2g

Fat: 2g

Fiber: 4g

133. CARROT COOLER:

Time: 5 mins

Servings: 2

INGREDIENTS:

- 2 Big carrots, peel off and chop-up
- 1 apple, cored and chop-up
- 1-inch piece of ginger, peel off
- 1 cup of coconut water
- Ice cubes

INSTRUCTIONS:

1. Blend the items together in a blender.

2. Blend everything thoroughly up to it's smooth.

3. When the appropriate consistency is attained, add ice cubes and mix once more.

4. Pour cold liquid into glasses and serve.

NUTRITION INFO (PER SERVING):

Cals: 80

Carbs: 20g

Protein: 1g

Fat: 0g

Fiber: 4g

134.BEETROOT BEAUTY:

Time: 5 mins

Servings: 1

INGREDIENTS:

- 1 mini beetroot, peel off and chop-up
- 1 cup of pineapple chunks
- 1 cup of coconut water
- 1 tbsp lime juice
- 1 tbsp honey or agave syrup (non-compulsory)
- Ice cubes

INSTRUCTIONS:

1. Blend the items together in a blender.

2. Blend everything thoroughly up to it's smooth.

3. When the appropriate consistency is attained, add ice cubes and mix once more.

4. Pour cold liquid into a glass and serve.

NUTRITION INFO (PER SERVING):

Cals: 120

Carbs: 30g

Protein: 2g

Fat: 0.5g

Fiber: 5g

135. PINEAPPLE PASSION:

Time: 5 mins

Servings: 2

INGREDIENTS:

- 2 cups of pineapple chunks
- 1 cup of coconut milk
- 1 tbsp lime juice
- 1 tbsp honey or agave syrup (non-compulsory)
- Ice cubes

INSTRUCTIONS:

1. Blend the items together in a blender.

2. Blend till creamy and smooth.

3. When the appropriate consistency is attained, add ice cubes and mix once more.

4. Pour cold liquid into glasses and serve.

NUTRITION INFO (PER SERVING):

Cals: 180

Carbs: 40g

Protein: 1g

Fat: 3g

Fiber: 4g

136.MANGO MARVEL:

Time: 5 mins

Servings: 2

INGREDIENTS:

- 2 ripe mangoes, peel off and chop-up
- 1 cup of almond milk
- 1 tbsp lime juice
- 1 tbsp honey or maple syrup (non-compulsory)
- Ice cubes

INSTRUCTIONS:

1. In a blender, mix all the ingredients.

2. Blend up to well-mixd and creamy.

3. Once you've gotten the correct consistency, add ice cubes and blend once more.

4. Serve chilled after pouring into glasses.

NUTRITION INFO (PER SERVING):

Cals: 180

Carbs: 40g

Protein: 3g

Fat: 2g

Fiber: 4g

137.WATERMELON CRUSH:

Time: 5 mins

Servings: 2

INGREDIENTS:

- 4 cups of watermelon cubes
- 1 tbsp lime juice
- 1 tbsp honey or agave syrup (non-compulsory)
- Ice cubes

INSTRUCTIONS:

1. Blend the items together in a blender.

2. Blend everything thoroughly up to it's smooth.

3. When the appropriate consistency is attained, add ice cubes and mix once more.

4. Pour cold liquid into glasses and serve.

NUTRITION INFO (PER SERVING):

Cals: 80

Carbs: 20g

Protein: 1g

Fat: 0g

Fiber: 2g

138.GINGER FIRE

Time: 10 mins

Servings: 2

INGREDIENTS:

- 2 cups of water
- 1 tbsp finely grated ginger
- 2 tbsp honey
- Juice of 1 lemon
- 1/4 tsp cayenne pepper

INSTRUCTIONS:

1. Bring water to a rolling boil in a mini saucepan.

2. To the boiling water, add the finely grated ginger, and then simmer for five mins.

3. Take out the ginger-infused water from the heat and pour it into a pitcher.

4. Add honey, lemon juice, and cayenne pepper; mix thoroughly.

5. You can serve the Ginger Fire beverage warm or cold.

NUTRITION INFO (PER SERVING):

Cals: 40

Carbs: 11g

Fat: 0g

Protein: 0g

139.POMEGRANATE PUNCH

Time: 15 mins

Servings: 4

INGREDIENTS:

- 2 cups of pomegranate juice
- 1 cup of orange juice
- 1 cup of pineapple juice
- 1 cup of sparkling water
- Ice cubes
- Fresh mint leaves (for garnish)

INSTRUCTIONS:

1. Pomegranate juice, orange juice, and pineapple juice Must all be mixd in a pitcher.

2. Add sparkling water and stir.

3. To individual glasses, add ice cubes. Then, pour the pomegranate punch over the ice.

4. Serve with fresh mint leaves as a garnish.

NUTRITION INFO (PER SERVING):

Cals: 120

Carbs: 30g

Fat: 0g

Protein: 1g

140.BLUEBERRY BLAST

Time: 5 mins

Servings: 1

INGREDIENTS:

- 1 cup of blueberries
- 1/2 cup of plain yogurt
- 1/2 cup of almond milk
- 1 tbsp honey
- Ice cubes

INSTRUCTIONS:

1. Blend blueberries, plain yogurt, almond milk, honey, and a few ice cubes together in a blender.

2. Blend till creamy and smooth.

3. The Blueberry Blast Must be poured into a cold glass and served.

NUTRITION INFO (PER SERVING):

Cals: 170

Carbs: 34g

Fat: 3g

Protein: 5g

141.RASPBERRY RAPTURE

Time: 10 mins

Servings: 2

INGREDIENTS:

- 2 cups of raspberries
- 1 cup of coconut water
- 1/2 cup of orange juice
- 1 tbsp lime juice
- 1 tbsp agave syrup
- Ice cubes

INSTRUCTIONS:

1. Raspberries, coconut water, orange juice, lime juice, agave syrup, and a few ice cubes Must all be blended together.

2. Up to smooth, blend.

3. Place glasses with the Raspberry Rapture in them and serve cold.

NUTRITION INFO (PER SERVING):

Cals: 100

Carbs: 24g

Fat: 1g

Protein: 2g

142.CREAMY COCONUT

Time: 5 mins

Servings: 1

INGREDIENTS:

- 1 cup of coconut milk
- 1/2 cup of pineapple chunks
- 1 ripe banana
- 1 tbsp shredded coconut
- Ice cubes

INSTRUCTIONS:

1. Coconut milk, pineapple chunks, ripe bananas, shredded coconut, and a few ice cubes Must all be blended together.

2. Blend till creamy and smooth.

3. Place the cooled Creamy Coconut beverage in a glass and serve.

NUTRITION INFO (PER SERVING):

Cals: 290

Carbs: 36g

Fat: 18g

Protein: 3g

143.KIWI FUSION

Time: 5 mins

Servings: 1

INGREDIENTS:

- 2 kiwis, peel off and split
- 1/2 cup of cucumber, peel off and split
- 1/2 cup of spinach
- 1/2 cup of coconut water
- 1 tbsp lime juice
- Ice cubes

INSTRUCTIONS:

1. Kiwis, cucumber, spinach, coconut water, lime juice, and a few ice cubes Must all be mixd in a blender.

2. Up to smooth, blend.

3. Place chilled Kiwi Fusion in a glass and serve.

NUTRITION INFO (PER SERVING):

Cals: 90

Carbs: 20g

Fat: 1g

Protein: 3g

144.PEAR PERK

Time: 10 mins

Servings: 2

INGREDIENTS:

- 2 ripe pears, peel off and split
- 1 cup of almond milk
- 1 tbsp honey
- 1/4 tsp cinnamon
- Ice cubes

INSTRUCTIONS:

1. Ripe pears, almond milk, honey, cinnamon, and a few ice cubes Must all be mixd in a blender.

2. Blend till creamy and smooth.

3. Pear Perk Must be poured into chilled glasses and served.

NUTRITION INFO (PER SERVING):

Cals: 140

Carbs: 34g

Fat: 2g

Protein: 1g

145.PEVERYY PLEASURE

Time: 5 mins

Servings: 1

INGREDIENTS:

- 2 ripe peveryes, pitted and split
- 1/2 cup of Greek yogurt
- 1/2 cup of almond milk
- 1 tbsp honey
- Ice cubes

INSTRUCTIONS:

1. Blend ripe peveryes, Greek yogurt, almond milk, honey, and a few ice cubes in a blender.

2. Blend up to well-mixd and creamy.

3. Serving cold, pour the Peveryy Pleasure into a glass.

NUTRITION INFO (PER SERVING):

Cals: 200

Carbs: 42g

Fat: 3g

Protein: 8g

146. BEETROOT BLAST:

Time: 10 mins

Servings: 2

INGREDIENTS:

- 2 medium-sized beetroots, peel off and chop-up
- 1 cup of fresh orange juice
- 1 tbsp of honey (non-compulsory)
- Ice cubes (non-compulsory)

INSTRUCTIONS:

1. Juice from a fresh orange and diced beets Must be blended together.
2. Blend everything thoroughly up to it's smooth.
3. If honey is preferred, taste it and add.
4. Add some ice cubes and mix the mixture one more for a cold beverage.
5. Pour into glasses and start serving right away.

147. PINEAPPLE DELIGHT:

Time: 5 mins

Servings: 1

INGREDIENTS:

- 1 cup of fresh pineapple chunks
- 1/2 cup of coconut milk
- 1/2 cup of ice cubes
- 1 tbsp of honey (non-compulsory)

INSTRUCTIONS:

1. Put the coconut milk, ice cubes, pineapple pieces, and honey (if using) in a blender.
2. Blend till creamy and smooth.
3. Pour cold liquid into a glass and serve.

148.MANGO MADNESS:

Time: 8 mins

Servings: 2

INGREDIENTS:

- 2 ripe mangoes, peel off and diced
- 1 cup of unsweetened almond milk
- 1/2 cup of Greek yogurt
- 1 tbsp of lime juice
- 1 tbsp of honey (non-compulsory)

INSTRUCTIONS:

1. Mangoes that have been diced, almond milk, Greek yogurt, lime juice, and honey (if using) Must all be mixd in a blender.
2. Blend till creamy and smooth.
3. Pour cold liquid into glasses and serve.

149.WATERMELON WONDER:

Time: 5 mins

Servings: 2

INGREDIENTS:

- 2 cups of diced watermelon
- 1/2 cup of fresh mint leaves
- 1 tbsp of lime juice
- Ice cubes

INSTRUCTIONS:

1. Blend together some ice cubes, lime juice, mint leaves, and chop-up watermelon.
2. Blend everything thoroughly up to it's smooth.
3. Pour into glasses, add more mint leaves as a garnish if desired, and serve cold.

150. GINGER CRUSH:

Time: 10 mins

Servings: 1

INGREDIENTS:

- 1 tbsp of freshly finely grated ginger
- 1 cup of fresh orange juice
- 1 tbsp of honey (non-compulsory)
- Ice cubes

INSTRUCTIONS:

1. Blend the freshly finely grated ginger, fresh orange juice, and honey (if using) together in a blender.
2. Blend everything thoroughly.
3. To make it cold and foamy, add ice cubes and mix once more.
4. Pour into a glass, then serve right away.

151. POMEGRANATE PASSION:

Time: 5 mins

Servings: 1

INGREDIENTS:

- 1 cup of pomegranate seeds
- 1/2 cup of cranberry juice
- 1 tbsp of lime juice
- 1 tbsp of honey (non-compulsory)
- Ice cubes

INSTRUCTIONS:

1. In a blender, mix the pomegranate seeds, cranberry juice, lime juice, and honey (if using).

2. Blend everything thoroughly up to it's smooth.
3. When the mixture is cold, add ice cubes and mix again.
4. To serve, pour into a glass.

152.BLUEBERRY BREEZE:

Time: 7 mins

Servings: 2

INGREDIENTS:

- 1 cup of fresh blueberries
- 1 ripe banana
- 1/2 cup of almond milk
- 1/2 cup of Greek yogurt
- 1 tbsp of honey (non-compulsory)

INSTRUCTIONS:

1. Fresh blueberries, a ripe banana, almond milk, Greek yogurt, and honey (if using) Must all be put in a blender.
2. Blend till creamy and smooth.
3. Pour cold liquid into glasses and serve.

153.RASPBERRY REFRESH:

Time: 6 mins

Servings: 2

INGREDIENTS:

- 1 cup of fresh raspberries
- 1 cup of unsweetened coconut water
- 1 tbsp of lime juice
- Ice cubes

INSTRUCTIONS:

1. Blend up some ice cubes, fresh raspberries, coconut water, lime juice, and so on.

2. Blend everything thoroughly up to it's smooth.
3. Pour into glasses, add a few raspberries as a garnish if you like, and serve cold.

154. CREAMY DREAM:

Time: 8 mins

Servings: 1

INGREDIENTS:

- 1 ripe avocado
- 1 cup of almond milk
- 2 tbsp of cocoa powder
- 1 tbsp of honey or maple syrup
- Ice cubes

INSTRUCTIONS:

1. Blend the ripe avocado with the almond milk, chocolate, honey, or maple syrup, and ice cubes in a blender.
2. Blend up to smooth and creamy.
3. Pour cold liquid into a glass and serve.

155. KIWI SPARKLE:

Time: 5 mins

Servings: 1

INGREDIENTS:

- 2 ripe kiwis, peel off and split
- 1/2 cup of sparkling water
- 1 tbsp of lime juice
- Ice cubes

INSTRUCTIONS:

1. Blend together the kiwis, lime juice, sparkling water, and ice cubes.
2. Blend up to well-mixd and smooth.

3. Pour cold liquid into a glass and serve.

156.PEAR PLEASER

Time: 10 mins

Servings: 2

INGREDIENTS:

- 2 ripe pears
- 1 cup of almond milk
- 1 tbsp of honey
- 1 tsp of vanilla extract
- A pinch of cinnamon

INSTRUCTIONS:

1. Pears Must be peel off and cored before being slice into pieces.

2. The pears, almond milk, honey, cinnamon, and vanilla extract Must all be blended together.

3. Blend till creamy and smooth.

4. Pour cold liquid into glasses and serve.

NUTRITION INFO (PER SERVING):

Cals: 150

Carbs: 35g

Protein: 2g

Fat: 2g

Fiber: 5g

157.PEVERYY PUNCH

Time: 15 mins

Servings: 4

INGREDIENTS:

- 2 ripe peveryes
- 1 cup of orange juice
- 1 cup of pineapple juice
- 1 cup of sparkling water
- Fresh mint leaves for garnish (non-compulsory)

INSTRUCTIONS:

1. Split peveryes that have been peel off and pitted.

2. Slices of pevery, orange juice, and pineapple juice Must all be mixd in a blender.

3. Up to smooth, blend.

4. Then, add the sparkling water after pouring the mixture into a pitcher. Stir thoroughly.

5. If preferred, garnish with fresh mint leaves while serving over ice.

NUTRITION INFO (PER SERVING):

Cals: 120

Carbs: 30g

Protein: 1g

Fat: 0g

Fiber: 2g

158.STRAWBERRY SURPRISE

Time: 10 mins

Servings: 2

INGREDIENTS:

- 1 cup of fresh strawberries
- 1 cup of plain Greek yogurt
- 1 banana
- 1 tbsp of honey
- 1/2 cup of milk (any type)

INSTRUCTIONS:

1. Strawberry hulling and washing.

2. Blend the strawberries, Greek yogurt, banana, honey, and milk together in a blender.

3. Blend till creamy and smooth.

4. Pour cold liquid into glasses and serve.

NUTRITION INFO (PER SERVING):

Cals: 180

Carbs: 35g

Protein: 12g

Fat: 2g

Fiber: 4g

159.MELON MAGIC

Time: 5 mins

Servings: 2

INGREDIENTS:

- 2 cups of combined melon chunks (watermelon, honeydew, cantaloupe, etc.)
- 1/2 cup of coconut water
- Juice of 1 lime
- Fresh mint leaves for garnish (non-compulsory)

INSTRUCTIONS:

1. The chunks of combined melon, coconut water, and lime juice Must all be mixd in a blender.

2. Up to smooth, blend.

3. Pour into glasses and, if preferred, garnish with fresh mint leaves.

4. Offer cold.

NUTRITION INFO (PER SERVING):

Cals: 70

Carbs: 18g

Protein: 1g

Fat: 0g

Fiber: 2g

160.GOLDEN GLOW

Time: 10 mins

Servings: 1

INGREDIENTS:

- 1 ripe mango
- 1 mini orange
- 1 mini carrot
- 1/2 cup of coconut water
- 1 tbsp of chia seeds (non-compulsory)

INSTRUCTIONS:

1. The mango Must be peel off, pitted, and then chop-up.

2. Take out the orange's seeds after peeling.

3. Chop the carrot after peeling it.

4. Mango chunks, orange, carrot, coconut water, and chia seeds (if using) Must all be mixd in a blender.

5. Up to smooth, blend.

6. Pour cold liquid into a glass and serve.

NUTRITION INFO:

Cals: 220

Carbs: 50g

Protein: 4g

Fat: 3g

Fiber: 10g

161.MINTY COOL

Time: 5 mins

Servings: 2

INGREDIENTS:

- 2 cups of fresh cucumber, peel off and chop-up
- 1 cup of fresh mint leaves
- Juice of 1 lime
- 2 cups of cold water
- Ice cubes (non-compulsory)

INSTRUCTIONS:

1. Cucumber, mint leaves, lime juice, and water Must all be put in a blender.

2. Up to smooth, blend.

3. If you want a colder drink, add ice and mix one more.

4. Pour cold liquid into glasses and serve.

NUTRITION INFO (PER SERVING):

Cals: 25

Carbs: 6g

Protein: 1g

Fat: 0g

Fiber: 1g

162.GREEN ENERGY

Time: 10 mins

Servings: 1

INGREDIENTS:

- 1 green apple, cored and chop-up
- 1 cup of fresh spinach leaves
- 1/2 ripe avocado
- 1/2 cup of almond milk
- 1 tbsp of honey
- Juice of 1/2 lemon

INSTRUCTIONS:

1. The green apple, spinach, avocado, almond milk, honey, and lemon juice Must all be mixd in a blender.

2. Blend till creamy and smooth.

3. Pour cold liquid into a glass and serve.

NUTRITION INFO:

Cals: 250

Carbs: 36g

Protein: 6g

Fat: 12g

Fiber: 9g

163.BERRY BURST

Time: 10 mins

Servings: 2

INGREDIENTS:

- 1 cup of combined berries (strawberries, blueberries, raspberries)
- 1 cup of vanilla yogurt
- 1 banana
- 1 cup of milk (any type)
- 1 tbsp of honey

INSTRUCTIONS:

1. Berry cleaning.

2. The combined berries, yogurt, banana, milk, and honey Must all be blended together.

3. Blend till creamy and smooth.

4. Pour cold liquid into glasses and serve.

NUTRITION INFO (PER SERVING):

Cals: 200

Carbs: 42g

Protein: 6g

Fat: 3g

Fiber: 6g

164. CITRUS BLAST

Time: 5 mins

Servings: 1

INGREDIENTS:

- Juice of 2 oranges
- Juice of 1 grapefruit
- Juice of 1 lime
- 1 tbsp of agave syrup or honey
- Ice cubes (non-compulsory)

INSTRUCTIONS:

1. Squeeze the juice out of the lime, oranges, and grapefruit.

2. Blend the citrus juices with the honey or agave nectar in a blender.

3. Blend everything thoroughly.

4. If you want a colder drink, add ice and mix one more.

5. Pour cold liquid into a glass and serve.

NUTRITION INFO:

Cals: 120

Carbs: 30g

Protein: 2g

Fat: 0g

Fiber: 2g

165. VEGGIE INFUSION

Time: 10 mins

Servings: 2

INGREDIENTS:

- 1 medium-sized cucumber, peel off and chop-up
- 2 Big carrots, peel off and chop-up
- 2 stalks of celery, chop-up
- 1/2 lemon, peel off
- 2 cups of cold water
- Ice cubes (non-compulsory)

INSTRUCTIONS:

1. Blend the cucumber, carrots, celery, lemon, and water in a blender.

2. Up to smooth, blend.

3. If you want a colder drink, add ice and mix one more.

4. Pour cold liquid into glasses and serve.

NUTRITION INFO (PER SERVING):

Cals: 45

Carbs: 10g

Protein: 1g

Fat: 0g

Fiber: 3g

166.POWER PUNCH:

Time: 5 mins

Servings: 1

INGREDIENTS:

- 1 cup of spinach
- 1/2 cup of kale
- 1/2 cup of pineapple chunks
- 1/2 banana
- 1/2 cup of coconut water

INSTRUCTIONS:

1. Blend the items together in a blender.

2. Blend till creamy and smooth.

3. Serve right away.

NUTRITION INFO:

Cals: 180, Carbs: 42g, Protein: 5g, Fat: 1g

167.RAINBOW BLEND:

Time: 10 mins

Servings: 2

INGREDIENTS:

- 1/2 cup of strawberries
- 1/2 cup of blueberries
- 1/2 cup of chop-up mango
- 1/2 cup of chop-up kiwi
- 1/2 cup of chop-up pineapple
- 1 cup of almond milk

INSTRUCTIONS:

1. In a blender, mix all the ingredients.

2. Blend everything thoroughly up to it's smooth.

3. Pour cold liquid into glasses and serve.

NUTRITION INFO:

Cals: 140, Carbs: 30g, Protein: 2g, Fat: 3g

167.LEMONADE FIZZ:

Time: 15 mins

Servings: 4

INGREDIENTS:

- 4 lemons
- 4 cups of sparkling water
- 1/2 cup of honey
- Ice cubes

INSTRUCTIONS:

1. Lemon juice Must be squeezed and then strained to catch any seeds.

2. Mix the lemon juice, sparkling water, and honey in a pitcher. To thoroughly dissolve the honey, stir.

3. In every glass, place an ice cube before adding the lemonade.

4. If desired, add lemon slices as a garnish.

NUTRITION INFO:

Cals: 80, Carbs: 22g, Protein: 0g, Fat: 0g

168.ORANGE CRUSH:

Time: 5 mins

Servings: 1

INGREDIENTS:

- 2 oranges
- 1/2 cup of coconut water
- 1 tbsp honey (non-compulsory)
- Ice cubes

INSTRUCTIONS:

1. Orange juice Must be squeezed off the fruit and strained to catch any pulp.

2. Orange juice, coconut water, ice cubes, and honey (if using) Must all be blended together.

3. Blend up to foamy and well-mixd.

4. Pour cold liquid into a glass and serve.

NUTRITION INFO:

Cals: 120, Carbs: 28g, Protein: 2g, Fat: 0g

169.CARROT CRAZE:

Time: 8 mins

Servings: 2

INGREDIENTS:

- 2 Big carrots
- 1 apple
- 1/2 inch fresh ginger
- 1 cup of almond milk

- 1 tbsp honey (non-compulsory)

INSTRUCTIONS:

1. Apple and carrots Must be peel off and then slice into mini pieces.

2. Blend the carrots, apple, ginger, almond milk, and honey (if using) in a blender.

3. Blend till creamy and smooth.

4. Pour into glasses, then offer.

NUTRITION INFO:

Cals: 120, Carbs: 28g, Protein: 2g, Fat: 1g

170.BEETROOT BEAUTY:

Time: 10 mins

Servings: 2

INGREDIENTS:

- 1 medium-sized beetroot
- 1 apple
- 1/2 cup of strawberries
- 1/2 cup of Greek yogurt
- 1/2 cup of almond milk

INSTRUCTIONS:

1. Apple and beetroot Must be peel off and then slice into tiny pieces.

2. Blend the diced beetroot, apple, strawberries, Greek yogurt, and almond milk together in a blender.

3. Blend everything thoroughly up to it's smooth.

4. Pour cold liquid into glasses and serve.

NUTRITION INFO:

Cals: 150, Carbs: 28g, Protein: 8g, Fat: 2g

171.PINEAPPLE PARADISE:

Time: 5 mins

Servings: 1

INGREDIENTS:

- 1 cup of chop-up pineapple
- 1/2 cup of coconut milk
- 1/4 cup of orange juice
- 1/4 cup of Greek yogurt
- Ice cubes

INSTRUCTIONS:

1. Blend the items together in a blender.

2. Blend till creamy and smooth.

3. Pour cold liquid into a glass and serve.

NUTRITION INFO:

Cals: 180, Carbs: 40g, Protein: 4g, Fat: 3g

172.MANGO MANIA:

Time: 5 mins

Servings: 1

INGREDIENTS:

- 1 ripe mango
- 1/2 cup of pineapple chunks
- 1/2 cup of coconut water

- 1/4 cup of orange juice
- Ice cubes

INSTRUCTIONS:

1. Mangoes Must be peel off and slice into mini pieces.

2. In a blender, mix the chop-up mango, chunks of pineapple, coconut water, orange juice, and ice cubes.

3. Blend up to foamy and well-mixd.

4. Pour cold liquid into a glass and serve.

NUTRITION INFO:

Cals: 180, Carbs: 42g, Protein: 2g, Fat: 1g

173.WATERMELON SPLASH:

Time: 5 mins

Servings: 2

INGREDIENTS:

- 2 cups of chop-up watermelon
- 1/2 cup of fresh mint leaves
- 1 lime
- 1 cup of coconut water
- Ice cubes

INSTRUCTIONS:

1. In a blender, mix the diced up watermelon, mint leaves, lime juice, coconut water, and ice cubes.

2. Blend everything thoroughly up to it's smooth.

3. Pour cold liquid into glasses and serve.

174. GINGER ZING:

Time: 8 mins

Servings: 1

INGREDIENTS:

- 1 cup of chop-up pineapple
- 1/2 inch fresh ginger
- 1 tbsp lemon juice
- 1 tbsp honey
- 1 cup of water

INSTRUCTIONS:

1. The chop-up pineapple, fresh ginger, lemon juice, honey, and water Must all be put in a blender.
2. Blend up to foamy and well-mixd.
3. Pour cold liquid into a glass and serve.

175. PEAR PLEASURE:

Time: 15 mins

Servings: 2

INGREDIENTS:

- 2 ripe pears
- 1 cup of Greek yogurt
- 2 tbsp of honey
- 1/4 cup of granola
- Fresh mint leaves (for garnish)

INSTRUCTIONS:

1. Pears can be slice into cubes or thin slices.
2. Greek yogurt and honey Must be thoroughly blended in a bowl.
3. In bowls or serving glasses, arrange the pear slices or cubes in layers.
4. Overlay the pears with the yogurt mixture.
5. Over the yogurt, top with granola.
6. Use fresh mint leaves as a garnish.
7. Serve right away.

176.PEVERYY PARADISE:

Time: 10 mins

Servings: 2

INGREDIENTS:

- 2 ripe peveryes
- 1 cup of coconut milk
- 1 tbsp of agave syrup
- 1/2 tsp of vanilla extract
- Ice cubes

INSTRUCTIONS:

1. The peveryes Must be peel off, pitted, and then slice into pieces.
2. Blend the pevery chunks, coconut milk, agave syrup, vanilla essence, and a few ice cubes together in a blender.
3. Blend till creamy and smooth.
4. Pour into glasses and start serving right away.

177.STRAWBERRY SWIRL:

Time: 20 mins

Servings: 4

INGREDIENTS:

- 2 cups of refrigerate strawberries
- 1 cup of plain yogurt
- 2 tbsp of honey

- Fresh strawberries (for garnish)

INSTRUCTIONS:

1. The refrigerate strawberries, yogurt, and honey Must all be mixd in a blender.
2. Blend till creamy and smooth.
3. Place serving glasses with the mixture in them.
4. Swirl the mixture with a spoon or a skewer.
5. Use fresh strawberries as a garnish.
6. Serve right away.

178.MELON MADNESS:

Time: 15 mins

Servings: 2

INGREDIENTS:

- 1 cup of diced watermelon
- 1 cup of diced cantaloupe
- 1 cup of diced honeydew melon
- Juice of 1 lime
- Fresh mint leaves (for garnish)

INSTRUCTIONS:

1. The chop-up watermelon, cantaloupe, and honeydew melon Must be mixd in a bowl.
2. Add the lime juice to the melon mixture and toss it together gently.
3. The melon mixture Must be slice up among serving glasses or bowls.
4. Use fresh mint leaves as a garnish.
5. Offer cold.

179.GOLDEN GODDESS:

Time: 10 mins

Servings: 2

INGREDIENTS:

- 2 ripe bananas
- 1 cup of pineapple chunks
- 1 cup of mango chunks
- 1 cup of orange juice
- 1/2 cup of coconut water

INSTRUCTIONS:

1. Blend the ripe bananas, pineapple, mango, orange juice, and coconut water together in a blender.
2. Blend till creamy and smooth.
3. Pour into glasses and start serving right away.

180.MINTY FRESHNESS:

Time: 5 mins

Servings: 1

INGREDIENTS:

- 1 cup of fresh spinach
- 1 cup of fresh mint leaves
- 1/2 cup of cucumber slices
- 1/2 cup of pineapple chunks
- 1/2 cup of coconut water
- Ice cubes

INSTRUCTIONS:

1. Fresh spinach, mint leaves, cucumber slices, pineapple chunks, coconut water, and a few ice cubes Must all be put in a blender.
2. Blend everything thoroughly up to it's smooth.

3. Pour into a glass, then serve right away.

181. GREEN POWER:

Time: 10 mins

Servings: 2

INGREDIENTS:

- 2 cups of spinach
- 1 ripe avocado
- 1 cup of green grapes
- 1 cup of coconut water
- 1 tbsp of lemon juice

INSTRUCTIONS:

1. Blend the spinach, avocado, green grapes, coconut water, and lemon juice together in a blender.
2. Blend till creamy and smooth.
3. Pour into glasses and start serving right away.

182. BERRY BONANZA:

Time: 15 mins

Servings: 2

INGREDIENTS:

- 1 cup of combined berries (strawberries, blueberries, raspberries)
- 1 cup of almond milk
- 1/2 cup of plain Greek yogurt
- 1 tbsp of honey
- Ice cubes

INSTRUCTIONS:

1. Blend the combined berries, almond milk, Greek yogurt, honey, and a few ice cubes together in a blender.

2. Blend everything thoroughly up to it's smooth.
3. Pour into glasses and start serving right away.

183.CITRUS SYMPHONY:

Time: 10 mins

Servings: 2

INGREDIENTS:

- Juice of 2 oranges
- Juice of 1 grapefruit
- 1 tbsp of lemon juice
- 1 tbsp of lime juice
- 1 tbsp of honey
- Ice cubes

INSTRUCTIONS:

1. Orange juice, grapefruit juice, lemon juice, lime juice, honey, and a few ice cubes Must all be mixd in a pitcher.
2. After thoroughly combining, chill for a little while in the refrigerator.
3. Pour cold liquid into glasses and serve.

184.VEGGIE VITALITY:

Time: 15 mins

Servings: 2

INGREDIENTS:

- 2 Big carrots
- 1 cucumber
- 2 stalks of celery
- 1 green apple
- Juice of 1 lemon
- Ice cubes

INSTRUCTIONS:

1. Slice the cucumber and carrots into cubes after peeling them.
2. Slice the green apple and celery into mini pieces.
3. Juice the carrots, cucumber, celery, green apple, and lemon juice in a juicer or blender.
4. Blend everything thoroughly up to it's smooth.
5. Pour into glasses and start serving right away.

185.POWER FUEL

Time: 5 mins

Servings: 1

INGREDIENTS:

- 1 banana
- 1 cup of spinach
- 1 tbsp almond butter
- 1 cup of almond milk
- 1 tsp chia seeds

INSTRUCTIONS:

1. Put the banana in the blender after peeling it.

2. To the blender, add spinach, almond butter, almond milk, and chia seeds.

3. Blend every component up to it is creamy and smooth.

4. Pour into a glass, then sip.

NUTRITION INFO (PER SERVING):

Cals: 250

Protein: 8g

Carbs: 35g

Fat: 10g

Fiber: 9g

186.RAINBOW REFRESHER

Time: 10 mins

Servings: 2

INGREDIENTS:

- 1 cup of chop-up pineapple
- 1 cup of chop-up watermelon
- 1 cup of chop-up mango
- 1 cup of spinach
- 1 tbsp lime juice
- 1 cup of coconut water

INSTRUCTIONS:

1. Spinach, pineapple, watermelon, mango, lime juice, and coconut water Must all be mixd in a blender.

2. Blend everything thoroughly up to it's smooth.

3. Pour cold liquid into glasses and serve.

NUTRITION INFO (PER SERVING):

Cals: 120

Protein: 2g

Carbs: 30g

Fat: 0.5g

Fiber: 4g

187.LEMON LIME FIZZ

Time: 5 mins

Servings: 1

INGREDIENTS:

- Juice of 1 lemon
- Juice of 1 lime
- 1 tbsp honey
- Sparkling water

INSTRUCTIONS:

1. Honey, lime juice, and lemon juice Must all be mixd in a glass.

2. Stir the honey up to it dissolves.

3. Spritz some sparkling water into the glass.

4. Slices of lemon or lime may be used as a garnish.

5. Offer cold.

NUTRITION INFO (PER SERVING):

Cals: 40

Protein: 0g

Carbs: 12g

Fat: 0g

Fiber: 0g

188. ORANGE OASIS

Time: 5 mins

Servings: 1

INGREDIENTS:

- 1 orange
- 1/2 cup of coconut water
- 1/4 cup of Greek yogurt
- 1 tbsp honey

INSTRUCTIONS:

1. Take out the orange's seeds after peeling it.

2. Blend the orange with the Greek yogurt, honey, coconut water, and so forth.

3. Blend till creamy and smooth.

4. Pour into a glass, then sip.

NUTRITION INFO (PER SERVING):

Cals: 150

Protein: 6g

Carbs: 30g

Fat: 0.5g

Fiber: 4g

189.CARROT CRUNCH

Time: 15 mins

Servings: 2

INGREDIENTS:

- 2 Big carrots
- 1 tbsp olive oil
- 1 tsp paprika
- Salt and pepper as needed

INSTRUCTIONS:

1. The oven Must be set to 400°F (200°C).

2. Peeling and Cutting the carrots into sticks is necessary.

3. Olive oil, paprika, salt, and pepper Must all be mixd in a bowl before coating the carrot sticks completely.

4. Distribute the carrot sticks evenly on a baking sheet covered with parchment paper.

5. The carrots Must be cooked but still somewhat crisp after 10 to 12 mins in the oven.

6. Take them out of the oven and let them cool a bit before serving.

NUTRITION INFO (PER SERVING):

Cals: 80

Protein: 1g

Carbs: 8g

Fat: 5g

Fiber: 2g

190. BEETROOT BLAST

Time: 10 mins

Servings: 1

INGREDIENTS:

- 1 mini beetroot
- 1 cup of strawberries
- 1 cup of almond milk
- 1 tbsp honey

INSTRUCTIONS:

1. Beetroot Must be peel off and slice into mini pieces.

2. Beetroot, strawberries, almond milk, and honey Must all be put in a blender.

3. Blend everything thoroughly up to it's smooth.

4. Pour cold liquid into a glass and serve.

NUTRITION INFO (PER SERVING):

Cals: 150

Protein: 2g

Carbs: 30g

Fat: 3g

Fiber: 5g

191.PINEAPPLE PARTY

Time: 5 mins

Servings: 2

INGREDIENTS:

- 2 cups of chop-up pineapple
- 1 cup of coconut milk
- 1/2 cup of plain Greek yogurt
- 1 tbsp honey

INSTRUCTIONS:

1. Greek yogurt, honey, coconut milk, and diced pineapple Must all be blended together.
2. Blend till creamy and smooth.
3. Pour cold liquid into glasses and serve.

NUTRITION INFO (PER SERVING):

Cals: 180

Protein: 4g

Carbs: 30g

Fat: 5g

Fiber: 2g

192.MANGO MAGIC

Time: 5 mins

Servings: 1

INGREDIENTS:

- 1 ripe mango
- 1/2 cup of orange juice
- 1/2 cup of almond milk
- 1/4 tsp vanilla extract

INSTRUCTIONS:

1. Mangoes Must be peel off and slice into mini pieces.

2. Mango, orange juice, almond milk, and vanilla essence Must all be blended together.

3. Blend till creamy and smooth.

4. Pour into a glass, then sip.

NUTRITION INFO (PER SERVING):

Cals: 180

Protein: 2g

Carbs: 40g

Fat: 2g

Fiber: 3g

193.WATERMELON WAVE

Time: 5 mins

Servings: 2

INGREDIENTS:

- 4 cups of cubed watermelon
- Juice of 1 lime
- 1 tbsp honey
- Fresh mint leaves for garnish (non-compulsory)

INSTRUCTIONS:

1. Cubed watermelon, lime juice, and honey Must all be mixd in a blender.

2. Blend everything thoroughly up to it's smooth.

3. Pour into glasses and, if preferred, garnish with fresh mint leaves.

4. Offer cold.

NUTRITION INFO (PER SERVING):

Cals: 60

Protein: 1g

Carbs: 15g

Fat: 0g

Fiber: 1g

194.GINGER SNAP

Time: 10 mins

Servings: 1

INGREDIENTS:

- 1-inch piece of fresh ginger, peel off
- Juice of 1 lemon
- 1 tbsp honey
- 1 cup of sparkling water

INSTRUCTIONS:

1. Put some finely grated fresh ginger in a bowl.

2. Mix thoroughly after adding the honey and lemon juice to the bowl.

3. Pour the ginger-lemon combination and sparkling water into a glass.

4. Gently blend by stirring.

5. Offer cold.

NUTRITION INFO (PER SERVING):

Cals: 40

Protein: 0g

Carbs: 10g

Fat: 0g

Fiber: 0g

195.POMEGRANATE PLEASURE:

Time: 10 mins

Servings: 2

INGREDIENTS:

- 2 cups of pomegranate seeds
- 1 cup of plain Greek yogurt
- 1 tbsp honey

INSTRUCTIONS:

1. The pomegranate seeds, Greek yogurt, and honey Must all be mixd in a blender.

2. Blend till creamy and smooth.

3. Pour into serving glasses and, if preferred, top with more pomegranate seeds.

NUTRITION INFO PER SERVING:

Cals: 180

Protein: 10g

Fat: 2g

Carbs: 35g

Fiber: 5g

196.BLUEBERRY BLAST:

Time: 15 mins

Servings: 4

INGREDIENTS:

- 2 cups of blueberries
- 1 cup of almond milk
- 1 banana
- 1 tbsp chia seeds
- 1 tsp vanilla extract

INSTRUCTIONS:

1. Blend the items together in a blender.

2. Blend till creamy and smooth.

3. Pour cooled liquid into serving glasses.

NUTRITION INFO PER SERVING:

Cals: 120

Protein: 3g

Fat: 2g

Carbs: 25g

Fiber: 6g

197. RASPBERRY RIPPLE:

Time: 10 mins

Servings: 2

INGREDIENTS:

- 2 cups of raspberries
- 1 cup of coconut milk
- 1 tbsp agave syrup

INSTRUCTIONS:

1. The raspberries, coconut milk, and agave syrup Must all be mixd in a blender.

2. Up to smooth, blend.

3. Enjoy after pouring into serving glasses!

NUTRITION INFO PER SERVING:

Cals: 160

Protein: 2g

Fat: 8g

Carbs: 22g

Fiber: 8g

198.CREAMSICLE CREAMINESS:

Time: 10 mins

Servings: 2

INGREDIENTS:

- 2 oranges
- 1 cup of vanilla ice cream
- 1/2 cup of milk

INSTRUCTIONS:

1. Oranges are juiced, and the juice is then added to a blender.

2. The milk and vanilla ice cream Must be added to the blender.

3. Blend till creamy and smooth.

4. Pour into glasses for serving and start serving right away.

NUTRITION INFO PER SERVING:

Cals: 210

Protein: 4g

Fat: 8g

Carbs: 32g

Fiber: 2g

199. KIWI KISS:

Time: 10 mins

Servings: 2

INGREDIENTS:

- 4 kiwis
- 1 cup of pineapple chunks
- 1 cup of coconut water

INSTRUCTIONS:

1. Peel and slice the kiwis.

2. Put the kiwis, pineapple pieces, and coconut water in a blender.

3. Up to smooth, blend.

4. Enjoy after pouring into serving glasses!

NUTRITION INFO PER SERVING:

Cals: 110

Protein: 2g

Fat: 1g

Carbs: 26g

Fiber: 6g

200.PEAR PLEASURE:

Time: 10 mins

Servings: 2

INGREDIENTS:

- 2 ripe pears
- 1 cup of spinach
- 1/2 cup of almond milk
- 1 tbsp honey

INSTRUCTIONS:

1. Pears are peel off and chop-up.

2. Blend the pears, spinach, almond milk, and honey together in a blender.

3. Blend till creamy and smooth.

4. Enjoy after pouring into serving glasses!

NUTRITION INFO PER SERVING:

Cals: 130

Protein: 2g

Fat: 1g

Carbs: 32g

Fiber: 6g

201.PEVERYY PASSION:

Time: 10 mins

Servings: 2

INGREDIENTS:

- 2 ripe peveryes
- 1 cup of orange juice
- 1/2 cup of Greek yogurt
- 1 tbsp maple syrup

INSTRUCTIONS:

1. Peveryes Must be peel off and pitted before being chop-up.

2. Blend the peveryes, orange juice, Greek yogurt, and maple syrup in a blender.

3. Blend till creamy and smooth.

4. Pour cooled liquid into serving glasses.

NUTRITION INFO PER SERVING:

Cals: 180

Protein: 6g

Fat: 1g

Carbs: 38g

Fiber: 3g

202.STRAWBERRY SWIRL:

Time: 10 mins

Servings: 2

INGREDIENTS:

- 2 cups of strawberries
- 1 cup of coconut milk
- 1 tbsp honey

INSTRUCTIONS:

1. Strawberries, coconut milk, and honey Must all be blended together.

2. Up to smooth, blend.

3. Enjoy after pouring into serving glasses!

NUTRITION INFO PER SERVING:

Cals: 140

Protein: 2g

Fat: 5g

Carbs: 25g

Fiber: 7g

203. MELON MEDLEY:

Time: 10 mins

Servings: 2

INGREDIENTS:

- 2 cups of combined melon chunks (watermelon, honeydew, cantaloupe)
- 1 cup of coconut water
- Juice of 1 lime

INSTRUCTIONS:

1. The chunks of combined melon, coconut water, and lime juice Must all be mixd in a blender.

2. Up to smooth, blend.

3. Pour cooled liquid into serving glasses.

NUTRITION INFO PER SERVING:

Cals: 80

Protein: 1g

Fat: 0g

Carbs: 20g

Fiber: 2g

204. GOLDEN SUNSHINE:

Time: 10 mins

Servings: 2

INGREDIENTS:

- 2 oranges
- 1 mango, peel off and pitted
- 1/2 cup of pineapple chunks
- 1/2 cup of carrot juice

INSTRUCTIONS:

1. Oranges are juiced, and the juice is then added to a blender.

2. Mango, pineapple pieces, and carrot juice Must all be added to the blender.

3. Up to smooth, blend.

4. Enjoy after pouring into serving glasses!

NUTRITION INFO PER SERVING:

Cals: 150

Protein: 2g

Fat: 1g

Carbs: 37g

Fiber: 4g

205.MINT MOJITO:

Time: 5 mins

Servings: 1

INGREDIENTS:

- 10 fresh mint leaves
- 2 tsp sugar
- Juice of 1 lime
- 1/2 cup of club soda
- Ice cubes

INSTRUCTIONS:

1. Mint leaves and sugar Must be muddled in a glass to release the mint's scent.
2. Stir well after adding lime juice.
3. Ice cubes are added to the glass, then club soda is added on top.
4. Garnish with a mint sprig after a gentle stir. Use refrigerated food.

206.GREEN REVIVAL:

Time: 10 mins

Servings: 2

INGREDIENTS:

- 2 cups of spinach
- 1 cup of cucumber, chop-up
- 1 green apple, cored and chop-up
- 1/2 lemon, juiced
- 1 cup of coconut water
- Ice cubes

INSTRUCTIONS:

1. Blend spinach, cucumber, green apple, lemon juice, and coconut water in a food processor.
2. Up to smooth, blend.
3. When the appropriate consistency is attained, add ice cubes and mix once more.
4. Pour cold liquid into glasses and serve.

207.BERRY BOOST:

Time: 5 mins

Servings: 1

INGREDIENTS:

- 1 cup of combined berries (strawberries, blueberries, raspberries)
- 1/2 cup of plain yogurt
- 1 tbsp honey
- 1/2 cup of almond milk
- Ice cubes

INSTRUCTIONS:

1. Almond milk, yogurt, honey, and combined berries Must all be mixd in a blender.
2. Up to smooth, blend.
3. When the appropriate consistency is attained, add ice cubes and mix once more.
4. Pour cold liquid into a glass and serve.

208.CITRUS SYMPHONY:

Time: 5 mins

Servings: 1

INGREDIENTS:

- Juice of 1 orange
- Juice of 1 grapefruit
- Juice of 1 lemon
- 1 tbsp honey
- 1/2 cup of sparkling water
- Ice cubes

INSTRUCTIONS:

1. Orange juice, grapefruit juice, lemon juice, and honey Must all be mixd in a glass.
2. Up to honey is dissolved, stir thoroughly.
3. Add ice cubes and sparkling water.
4. Gently stir, then serve cold.

209.VEGGIE DELIGHT:

Time: 15 mins

Servings: 2

INGREDIENTS:

- 2 Big carrots, peel off and chop-up
- 1 cucumber, chop-up
- 2 celery stalks, chop-up
- 1/2 lemon, juiced
- 1/2 inch fresh ginger, finely grated
- 1 cup of water
- Ice cubes

INSTRUCTIONS:

1. Blend carrots, cucumber, celery, water, lemon juice, and ginger in a blender.
2. Up to smooth, blend.
3. When the appropriate consistency is attained, add ice cubes and mix once more.
4. Pour cold liquid into glasses and serve.

210.POWER POTION:

Time: 5 mins

Servings: 1

INGREDIENTS:

- 1 banana
- 1 cup of spinach
- 1 tbsp peanut butter
- 1 cup of almond milk
- 1 tbsp chia seeds
- Ice cubes

INSTRUCTIONS:

1. Banana, spinach, peanut butter, almond milk, and chia seeds Must all be mixd in a blender.
2. Up to smooth, blend.
3. When the appropriate consistency is attained, add ice cubes and mix once more.
4. Pour cold liquid into a glass and serve.

211.RAINBOW RIOT:

Time: 10 mins

Servings: 2

INGREDIENTS:

1. 1 cup of pineapple chunks
2. 1 cup of mango chunks
3. 1 cup of strawberries, hulled
4. 1 cup of blueberries
5. 1 cup of coconut water
6. Ice cubes

INSTRUCTIONS:

1. Strawberries, blueberries, mango pieces, pineapple chunks, and coconut water Must all be mixd in a blender.
2. Up to smooth, blend.
3. When the appropriate consistency is attained, add ice cubes and mix once more.
4. Pour cold liquid into glasses and serve.

212.LEMON LIME FUSION:

Time: 5 mins

Servings: 1

INGREDIENTS:

- Juice of 1 lemon
- Juice of 1 lime
- 1 tbsp agave syrup
- 1 cup of sparkling water
- Ice cubes

INSTRUCTIONS:

1. Lemon juice, lime juice, and agave syrup Must all be mixd in a glass.
2. Once the syrup has dissolved, stir thoroughly.

3. Add ice cubes and sparkling water.
4. Gently stir, then serve cold.

213. ORANGE OASIS:

Time: 5 mins

Servings: 1

INGREDIENTS:

- Juice of 2 oranges
- 1/2 cup of pineapple juice
- 1/4 cup of coconut milk
- 1/2 tsp vanilla extract
- Ice cubes

INSTRUCTIONS:

1. Orange juice, pineapple juice, coconut milk, and vanilla essence Must all be mixd in a glass.
2. Once all the ingredients are mixd, thoroughly stir.
3. Re-stir, then add the ice cubes.
4. Offer cold.

214. CARROT CRAZE:

Time: 10 mins

Servings: 2

INGREDIENTS:

- 2 Big carrots, peel off and chop-up
- 1 orange, peel off and segmented
- 1/2 cup of Greek yogurt
- 1 tbsp honey
- 1/2 tsp ground cinnamon
- Ice cubes

INSTRUCTIONS:

1. Blend carrots, orange segments, Greek yogurt, honey, and cinnamon in a food processor.
2. Up to smooth, blend.
3. When the appropriate consistency is attained, add ice cubes and mix once more.
4. Pour cold liquid into glasses and serve.

215.BEETROOT BLISS

Time: 10 mins

Servings: 2

INGREDIENTS:

- 2 medium-sized beetroots, peel off and chop-up
- 1 medium-sized apple, cored and chop-up
- 1 cup of coconut water
- 1 tbsp lemon juice
- 1 tsp honey (non-compulsory)
- Ice cubes (non-compulsory)

INSTRUCTIONS:

1. Blend the apple, coconut water, lemon juice, honey (if used), and diced beetroot in the blender.
2. Blend till creamy and smooth.
3. Ice cubes may be added if preferred. Blend again up to thoroughly blended.
4. Place cold drinks in glasses after pouring the mixture.

NUTRITION INFO:

Cals: 120

Carbs: 28g

Protein: 2g

Fat: 0.5g

Fiber: 5g

216.PINEAPPLE PARADISE

Time: 5 mins

Servings: 1

INGREDIENTS:

- 1 cup of fresh pineapple chunks
- 1/2 cup of coconut milk
- 1/2 cup of orange juice
- 1/4 tsp vanilla extract
- Ice cubes

INSTRUCTIONS:

1. Blend together the ice cubes, coconut milk, orange juice, vanilla essence, and pineapple chunks.

2. Blend up to foamy and well-mixd.

3. Place the cold mixture in a glass and serve.

NUTRITION INFO:

Cals: 180

Carbs: 40g

Protein: 2g

Fat: 4g

Fiber: 3g

217.MANGO MAGIC

Time: 8 mins

Servings: 2

INGREDIENTS:

- 1 ripe mango, peel off and chop-up
- 1/2 cup of plain yogurt
- 1/2 cup of orange juice
- 1/2 cup of almond milk (or any other milk of your choice)
- 1 tbsp honey (non-compulsory)
- Ice cubes

INSTRUCTIONS:

1. Blend together the mango chunks, yogurt, orange juice, almond milk, and honey (if using).

2. Blend till creamy and smooth.

3. Once more blending is complete, add some ice cubes.

4. Place cold drinks in glasses after pouring the mixture.

NUTRITION INFO:

Cals: 180

Carbs: 38g

Protein: 5g

Fat: 2g

Fiber: 3g

218.WATERMELON WHIRL

Time: 5 mins

Servings: 1

INGREDIENTS:

- 2 cups of fresh watermelon chunks
- 1/2 cup of cucumber, peel off and chop-up
- 1 tbsp lime juice
- Fresh mint leaves for garnish (non-compulsory)
- Ice cubes

INSTRUCTIONS:

1. Blend the cucumber, lime juice, watermelon chunks, and ice in a blender.

2. Blend everything thoroughly up to it's smooth.

3. Put a glass with the mixture inside.

4. If preferred, garnish with fresh mint leaves and serve cold.

NUTRITION INFO:

Cals: 80

Carbs: 20g

Protein: 2g

Fat: 0.5g

Fiber: 2g

219. GINGER SPICE

Time: 10 mins

Servings: 1

INGREDIENTS:

- 1 cup of unsweetened almond milk (or any other milk of your choice)
- 1 tsp finely grated fresh ginger
- 1 tsp honey (or maple syrup)
- 1/4 tsp ground cinnamon
- Pinch of ground nutmeg
- Pinch of ground cloves
- Pinch of black pepper
- Ice cubes

INSTRUCTIONS:

1. Almond milk, honey, finely grated ginger, cinnamon, nutmeg, cloves, and black pepper Must be heated in a mini saucepan over medium heat. As soon as the mixture is warm but not boiling, stir it occasionally.

2. Take it off the fire and give it a few mins to cool.

3. Add ice cubes to the mixture before pouring it into a blender.

4. Blend up to foamy and well-mixd.

5. Pour heated liquid into a cup of or glass.

NUTRITION INFO:

Cals: 70

Carbs: 10g

Protein: 1g

Fat: 3g

Fiber: 1g

220.POMEGRANATE POTION

Time: 15 mins

Servings: 2

INGREDIENTS:

- 2 cups of pomegranate arils
- 1 cup of cranberry juice
- 1 tbsp lemon juice
- 1 tbsp honey (non-compulsory)
- Ice cubes

INSTRUCTIONS:

1. Blend the pomegranate seeds, cranberry juice, honey (if using), and lemon juice together in a blender.

2. Blend everything thoroughly up to it's smooth.

3. When the mixture is cold, add some ice cubes.

4. Serve the mixture by pouring it into glasses.

NUTRITION INFO:

Cals: 160

Carbs: 40g

Protein: 2g

Fat: 0.5g

Fiber: 5g

221.BLUEBERRY BURST

Time: 5 mins

Servings: 1

INGREDIENTS:

- 1 cup of refrigerate blueberries
- 1/2 cup of Greek yogurt
- 1/2 cup of almond milk (or any other milk of your choice)
- 1 tbsp honey (non-compulsory)
- Ice cubes

INSTRUCTIONS:

1. Blend together the Greek yogurt, almond milk, refrigerate blueberries, and honey (if using).

2. Blend till creamy and smooth.

3. Once more blending is complete, add some ice cubes.

4. Place the cold mixture in a glass and serve.

NUTRITION INFO:

Cals: 180

Carbs: 35g

Protein: 8g

Fat: 3g

Fiber: 6g

222.RASPBERRY RHAPSODY

Time: 8 mins

Servings: 2

INGREDIENTS:

- 1 cup of fresh raspberries
- 1 cup of coconut water
- 1/2 cup of plain yogurt
- 1 tbsp honey (non-compulsory)
- Ice cubes

INSTRUCTIONS:

1. Blend together the raspberries, coconut water, plain yogurt, and any additional honey you're using.

2. Blend till creamy and smooth.

3. Once more blending is complete, add some ice cubes.

4. Place cold drinks in glasses after pouring the mixture.

NUTRITION INFO:

Cals: 120

Carbs: 25g

Protein: 3g

Fat: 1g

Fiber: 8g

223. CREAMY CITRUS

Time: 5 mins

Servings: 1

INGREDIENTS:

- 1 orange, peel off and segmented
- 1/2 cup of Greek yogurt
- 1/4 cup of orange juice
- 1 tbsp honey (non-compulsory)
- Ice cubes

INSTRUCTIONS:

1. Blend together the orange segments, Greek yogurt, orange juice, and any additional honey you're using.

2. Blend till creamy and smooth.

3. Once more blending is complete, add some ice cubes.

4. Place the cold mixture in a glass and serve.

NUTRITION INFO:

Cals: 160

Carbs: 30g

Protein: 10g

Fat: 0.5g

Fiber: 4g

224.KIWI DELIGHT

Time: 5 mins

Servings: 1

INGREDIENTS:

- 2 kiwis, peel off and chop-up
- 1/2 cup of pineapple juice
- 1/2 cup of coconut water
- 1 tbsp lime juice
- Ice cubes

INSTRUCTIONS:

1. Blend together the kiwis that have been slice, pineapple juice, coconut water, lime juice, and ice cubes.

2. Blend everything thoroughly up to it's smooth.

3. Place the cold mixture in a glass and serve.

NUTRITION INFO:

Cals: 120

Carbs: 28g

Protein: 2g

Fat: 0.5g

Fiber: 5g

225.PEAR PARADISE:

Time: 10 mins

Servings: 2

INGREDIENTS:

- 2 ripe pears
- 1 cup of almond milk
- 1 tbsp honey
- 1/2 tsp vanilla extract

INSTRUCTIONS:

1. Pears Must be peel off and cored before being slice into pieces.
2. Pears, almond milk, honey, and vanilla extract Must all be blended together.
3. Blend till creamy and smooth.
4. Pour into glasses, then offer.

226.PEVERY PERFECTION:

Time: 5 mins

Servings: 1

INGREDIENTS:

- 1 ripe pevery
- 1/2 cup of Greek yogurt
- 1/4 cup of orange juice
- 1 tbsp honey

INSTRUCTIONS:

1. Slice the pevery after it has been peel off and pitted.
2. Slices of pevery, Greek yogurt, orange juice, and honey Must all be mixd in a blender.
3. Blend till creamy and smooth.
4. Place in a glass and sip.

227. STRAWBERRY SMOOTHIE:

Time: 5 mins

Servings: 2

INGREDIENTS:

- 2 cups of fresh strawberries
- 1 banana
- 1 cup of milk (dairy or plant-based)
- 1 tbsp honey

INSTRUCTIONS:

1. Slice the banana and hull the strawberries.
2. Blend the strawberries, banana, milk, and honey together in a blender.
3. Blend till creamy and smooth.
4. Pour cold liquid into glasses and serve.

228. MELON MANIA:

Time: 10 mins

Servings: 2

INGREDIENTS:

- 2 cups of diced combined melons (watermelon, cantaloupe, honeydew)
- 1/2 cup of coconut water
- Juice of 1 lime
- 1 tbsp fresh mint leaves

INSTRUCTIONS:

1. The split melons, coconut water, lime juice, and mint leaves Must all be blended together.
2. Blend everything thoroughly up to it's smooth.
3. Pour into glasses and, if preferred, top with more mint leaves.
4. Offer cold.

229.GOLDEN ELIXIR:

Time: 5 mins

Servings: 1

INGREDIENTS:

- 1 Big ripe mango
- 1 cup of orange juice
- 1/2 tsp turmeric powder
- 1/2 tsp finely grated ginger

INSTRUCTIONS:

1. Slice up the mango.
2. Mango, orange juice, turmeric powder, and ginger shavings Must all be mixd in a blender.
3. Blend everything thoroughly up to it's smooth.
4. Pour cold liquid into a glass and serve.

30.MINT MARVEL:

Time: 5 mins

Servings: 2

INGREDIENTS:

- 2 cups of fresh spinach leaves
- 1 cup of cucumber, chop-up
- 1/2 cup of fresh mint leaves
- 1 green apple, cored and chop-up
- Juice of 1 lime
- 1 cup of water

INSTRUCTIONS:

1. The spinach leaves, cucumber, mint leaves, green apple, lime juice, and water Must all be mixd in a blender.
2. Blend everything thoroughly up to it's smooth.

3. Pour cold liquid into glasses and serve.

231. GREEN GARDEN:

Time: 5 mins

Servings: 1

INGREDIENTS:

- 1 cup of kale leaves
- 1/2 cup of fresh parsley
- 1 green apple, cored and chop-up
- 1/2 cup of coconut water
- 1 tbsp lemon juice
- 1 tbsp honey

INSTRUCTIONS:

1. The kale leaves, parsley, green apple, coconut water, lemon juice, and honey Must all be mixd in a blender.
2. Blend everything thoroughly up to it's smooth.
3. Pour cold liquid into a glass and serve.

232. BERRY BOOST:

Time: 5 mins

Servings: 2

INGREDIENTS:

- 1 cup of combined berries (strawberries, blueberries, raspberries)
- 1 banana
- 1 cup of almond milk
- 1 tbsp chia seeds
- 1 tbsp honey

1. The combined berries, banana, almond milk, chia seeds, and honey Must all be mixd in a blender.
2. Blend everything thoroughly up to it's smooth.
3. Pour cold liquid into glasses and serve.

233. CITRUS DELIGHT:

Time: 5 mins

Servings: 1

INGREDIENTS:

- 1 orange
- 1 grapefruit
- 1/2 lemon
- 1/2 lime
- 1 tbsp honey

INSTRUCTIONS:

1. Juice the lime, lemon, orange, and grapefruit.
2. Blend the honey and citrus juices in a blender.
3. Blend everything thoroughly.
4. Pour cold liquid into a glass and serve.

234. VEGGIE HEAVEN:

Time: 10 mins

Servings: 2

INGREDIENTS:

- 1 Big carrot, peel off and chop-up
- 1 mini beet, peel off and chop-up
- 1 stalk celery, chop-up
- 1 cup of spinach leaves
- 1 cup of coconut water

- Juice of 1 lemon

INSTRUCTIONS:

1. Blend the carrot, beet, celery, spinach leaves, coconut water, and lemon juice together in a blender.
2. Blend everything thoroughly up to it's smooth.
3. Pour cold liquid into glasses and serve.

235.POWER BLEND

Time: 5 mins

Servings: 1

INGREDIENTS:

- 1 cup of spinach
- 1/2 cup of kale
- 1 banana
- 1/2 cup of almond milk
- 1 tbsp chia seeds
- 1/2 cup of Greek yogurt

INSTRUCTIONS:

1. To a blender, add all the ingredients.

2. Blend till creamy and smooth.

3. Dispense and savor!

NUTRITION INFO:

Cals: 250

Protein: 15g

Carbs: 40g

Fat: 7g

Fiber: 10g

236.RAINBOW SPLASH

Time: 10 mins

Servings: 2

INGREDIENTS:

- 1 cup of chop-up watermelon
- 1/2 cup of diced pineapple
- 1/2 cup of split strawberries
- 1/2 cup of blueberries
- 1/2 cup of raspberries
- 1 cup of coconut water
- 1 tbsp honey (non-compulsory)

INSTRUCTIONS:

1. Mix all the ingredients in a blender.

2. Up to smooth, blend.

3. If honey is preferred, taste it and add.

4. Pour cold liquid into glasses and serve.

NUTRITION INFO:

Cals: 120

Protein: 2g

Carbs: 30g

Fat: 1g

Fiber: 6g

237. LEMONADE TWIST

Time: 15 mins

Servings: 4

INGREDIENTS:

- 4 lemons
- 4 cups of water
- 1/4 cup of honey or sugar
- Fresh mint leaves (non-compulsory)

INSTRUCTIONS:

1. Lemon juice Must be squeezed into a pitcher.

2. Fill the pitcher with water and sugar or honey.

3. Once the sweetener has dissolved, thoroughly stir.

4. For added flavor, add a few fresh mint leaves (non-compulsory).

5. Chill in the refrigerator for at least one hr.

6. Serve over ice and top with lemon or mint slices for decoration.

NUTRITION INFO:

Cals: 40

Protein: 0g

Carbs: 12g

Fat: 0g

Fiber: 0g

238.ORANGE DELIGHT

Time: 5 mins

Servings: 1

INGREDIENTS:

- 2 oranges
- 1/2 cup of Greek yogurt
- 1 tbsp honey (non-compulsory)
- Ice cubes

INSTRUCTIONS:

1. Oranges Must be seedless and peel off.

2. Blend the oranges with the Greek yogurt and honey, if using.

3. For a cool, refreshing chill, add a couple ice cubes.

4. Blend till creamy and smooth.

5. To serve, pour into a glass.

NUTRITION INFO:

Cals: 170

Protein: 9g

Carbs: 33g

Fat: 0g

Fiber: 4g

239.CARROT COOLER

Time: 10 mins

Servings: 2

INGREDIENTS:

- 2 Big carrots
- 1 apple
- 1/2 inch fresh ginger
- 1/2 cup of orange juice
- 1/2 cup of water
- Ice cubes

INSTRUCTIONS:

1. The carrots Must be washed, peel off, and then slice into little pieces.

2. Slice the apple into chunks after coring it.

3. Ginger Must be peel off and slice into minier pieces.

4. In a blender, mix the carrots, apple, ginger, orange juice, water, and ice cubes.

5. Up to smooth, blend.

6. Pour cold liquid into glasses and serve.

NUTRITION INFO:

Cals: 110

Protein: 1g

Carbs: 27g

Fat: 0g

Fiber: 4g

240.BEETROOT BEAUTY

Time: 8 mins

Servings: 1

INGREDIENTS:

- 1 mini beetroot, peel off and diced
- 1 medium carrot, peel off and diced
- 1 mini apple, cored and diced
- 1/2 cup of orange juice
- 1/2 cup of water
- 1 tsp lemon juice
- Ice cubes

INSTRUCTIONS:

1. Blend the diced apple, carrot, orange juice, water, lemon juice, and ice cubes in a blender with the beetroot and lemon juice.

2. Blend everything thoroughly up to it's smooth.

3. Pour cold liquid into a glass and serve.

NUTRITION INFO:

Cals: 140

Protein: 2g

Carbs: 32g

Fat: 0g

Fiber: 6g

241.PINEAPPLE PASSION

Time: 5 mins

Servings: 2

INGREDIENTS:

- 2 cups of fresh pineapple chunks
- 1 cup of coconut water
- 1/2 cup of plain Greek yogurt
- 1 tbsp honey (non-compulsory)
- Ice cubes

INSTRUCTIONS:

1. Blend the ice cubes, Greek yogurt, pineapple pieces, coconut water, and honey (if using) in a blender.

2. Blend till creamy and smooth.

3. Pour into glasses, then offer.

NUTRITION INFO:

Cals: 160

Protein: 6g

Carbs: 34g

Fat: 1g

Fiber: 3g

242. MANGO MARVEL

Time: 5 mins

Servings: 1

INGREDIENTS:

- 1 ripe mango, peel off and diced
- 1/2 cup of coconut milk
- 1/2 cup of orange juice
- 1/4 cup of plain Greek yogurt
- 1 tbsp honey (non-compulsory)
- Ice cubes

INSTRUCTIONS:

1. Blend together the diced mango, ice cubes, Greek yogurt, orange juice, coconut milk, and honey (if using).

2. Blend till creamy and smooth.

3. Pour cold liquid into a glass and serve.

NUTRITION INFO:

Cals: 220

Protein: 8g

Carbs: 44g

Fat: 4g

Fiber: 3g

243. WATERMELON CRUSH

Time: 5 mins

Servings: 2

INGREDIENTS:

- 2 cups of cubed watermelon
- 1/2 cup of fresh lime juice
- 1/4 cup of mint leaves
- 1 tbsp honey (non-compulsory)
- Ice cubes

INSTRUCTIONS:

1. Blend the watermelon cubes, lime juice, mint leaves, ice cubes, and honey (if using) in a blender.

2. Up to smooth, blend.

3. If necessary, add more honey after tasting to regulate the sweetness.

4. Pour cold liquid into glasses and serve.

NUTRITION INFO:

Cals: 80

Protein: 1g

Carbs: 20g

Fat: 0g

Fiber: 1g

244.GINGER FIRE

Time: 10 mins

Servings: 1

INGREDIENTS:

- 1 inch fresh ginger, peel off
- 1 mini apple, cored and split
- 1/2 lemon, juiced
- 1 tbsp honey
- 1 cup of water
- Ice cubes

INSTRUCTIONS:

1. Ginger Must be finely grated or chop-up lightly.

2. Blend the ginger, apple slices, lemon juice, honey, water, and ice cubes together in a blender.

3. Blend everything thoroughly and smoothly.

4. To serve, pour into a glass.

NUTRITION INFO:

Cals: 90

Protein: 0g

Carbs: 24g

Fat: 0g

Fiber: 2g

245.POMEGRANATE PUNCH:

Time: 10 mins

Servings: 4

INGREDIENTS:

- 2 cups of pomegranate juice
- 1 cup of orange juice
- 1 cup of sparkling water
- 1 tbsp honey (non-compulsory)
- Ice cubes
- Pomegranate seeds and orange slices for garnish (non-compulsory)

INSTRUCTIONS:

1. Pomegranate juice, orange juice, sparkling water, and honey (if using) Must all be mixd in a pitcher. Stir thoroughly.
2. Pour the punch over the ice after adding ice cubes to serving glasses.
3. If desired, garnish with orange slices and pomegranate seeds.
4. Enjoy while serving chilled!

246.BLUEBERRY BLAST:

Time: 5 mins

Servings: 2

INGREDIENTS:

- 1 cup of blueberries
- 1 cup of vanilla yogurt
- 1/2 cup of milk
- 1 tbsp honey (non-compulsory)
- Ice cubes

INSTRUCTIONS:

1. Blend blueberries, milk, vanilla yogurt, and honey (if using) in a food processor. Up to smooth, blend.
2. Pour the blueberry mixture over the ice in serving cups of that have been filled with ice cubes.
3. Gently stir, then serve cold.

247.RASPBERRY RAPTURE:

Time: 8 mins

Servings: 2

INGREDIENTS:

- 1 cup of raspberries
- 1 cup of coconut water
- 1/2 cup of pineapple juice
- 1 tbsp lime juice
- 1 tbsp agave syrup or honey
- Ice cubes

INSTRUCTIONS:

1. Blend together raspberries, coconut water, lime juice, pineapple juice, and agave syrup (or honey) in a food processor. Up to smooth, blend.
2. Pour the raspberry mixture over the ice in serving glasses that have been filled with ice cubes.
3. Gently stir, then serve cold.

248.CREAMY COCONUT:

Time: 5 mins

Servings: 1

INGREDIENTS:

- 1 cup of coconut milk
- 1/2 cup of pineapple chunks

- 1 ripe banana
- 1 tbsp shredded coconut
- Ice cubes

INSTRUCTIONS:

1. Coconut milk, pineapple chunks, bananas, and shredded coconut Must all be blended together. Up to smooth, blend.
2. Pour the creamy coconut mixture over the ice in a glass after adding ice cubes.
3. Gently stir, then serve cold.

249.KIWI FUSION:

Time: 10 mins

Servings: 2

INGREDIENTS:

- 2 ripe kiwis
- 1 cup of spinach leaves
- 1/2 cup of plain Greek yogurt
- 1/2 cup of apple juice
- 1 tbsp honey (non-compulsory)
- Ice cubes

INSTRUCTIONS:

1. Slice and peel the kiwis.
2. Kiwis, spinach leaves, Greek yogurt, apple juice, and honey (if wanted) Must all be mixd in a blender. Up to smooth, blend.
3. Place ice cubes in serving glasses before adding the kiwi mixture.
4. Gently stir, then serve cold.

250.PEAR PERK:

Time: 7 mins

Servings: 2

INGREDIENTS:

- 2 ripe pears
- 1 cup of almond milk
- 1/2 tsp vanilla extract
- 1 tbsp maple syrup or honey
- Ice cubes

INSTRUCTIONS:

1. Pears are peel off, cored, and chop-up.
2. Pears, almond milk, vanilla extract, and maple syrup (or honey) Must all be put in a blender. Up to smooth, blend.
3. Serving glasses with ice cubes Must be filled before adding the pear mixture.
4. Gently stir, then serve cold.

251.PEVERYY PLEASURE:

Time: 6 mins

Servings: 2

INGREDIENTS:

- 2 ripe peveryes
- 1 cup of coconut milk
- 1/2 cup of orange juice
- 1 tbsp lemon juice
- 1 tbsp agave syrup or honey
- Ice cubes

INSTRUCTIONS:

1. Slice, peel, and pit the peveryes.

2. Peveryes, coconut milk, orange juice, lemon juice, and agave syrup (or honey) Must all be put in a blender. Up to smooth, blend.
3. Serving cups of with ice cubes Must be filled before adding the pevery concoction.
4. Gently stir, then serve cold.

252.STRAWBERRY DELIGHT:

Time: 5 mins

Servings: 2

INGREDIENTS:

- 1 cup of strawberries
- 1 cup of milk
- 1/2 cup of vanilla ice cream
- 1 tbsp sugar or honey
- Ice cubes

INSTRUCTIONS:

1. Split strawberries that have been hulled.
2. Strawberries, milk, vanilla ice cream, sugar (or honey), and blender. Up to smooth, blend.
3. Pour the strawberry concoction over the ice in serving cups of that have been filled with ice cubes.
4. Gently stir, then serve cold.

253.MELON MINGLE:

Time: 8 mins

Servings: 4

INGREDIENTS:

- 2 cups of diced watermelon
- 1 cup of diced cantaloupe
- 1 cup of diced honeydew melon
- 1 cup of coconut water

- 1 tbsp lime juice
- 1 tbsp mint leaves, chop-up
- Ice cubes

INSTRUCTIONS:

1. Diced watermelon, cantaloupe, honeydew melon, coconut water, lime juice, and mint leaves, chop-up, Must all be mixd in a blender. Up to smooth, blend.
2. Serving cups of with ice cubes Must be filled before adding the melon mixture.
3. Gently stir, then serve cold.

254.GOLDEN GODDESS:

Time: 5 mins

Servings: 1

INGREDIENTS:

- 1 cup of mango chunks
- 1 cup of orange juice
- 1/2 cup of Greek yogurt
- 1 tbsp honey
- Ice cubes

INSTRUCTIONS:

1. Mango chunks, orange juice, Greek yogurt, and honey Must all be mixd in a blender. Up to smooth, blend.
2. Pour the golden goddess concoction over ice in a tumbler that has been filled with ice cubes.
3. Gently stir, then serve cold.

255.MINTY MELODY

Time: 10 mins

Servings: 2

INGREDIENTS:

- 2 cups of fresh mint leaves
- 1 cup of spinach
- 1 cucumber
- 1 green apple
- 1 lemon
- 1 tsp honey
- 1 cup of water

INSTRUCTIONS:

1. Thoroughly clean all the components.

2. Take out the cucumber's seeds after peeling it.

3. Slice the green apple, cucumber, and lemon.

4. Mint leaves, spinach, cucumber, green apple, lemon, honey, and water Must all be put in a blender.

5. Up to smooth, blend.

6. Offer cold.

NUTRITION INFO (PER SERVING):

Cals: 70

Fat: 0.5g

Carbs: 18g

Fiber: 4g

Protein: 2g

256.GREEN SYMPHONY

Time: 15 mins

Servings: 2

INGREDIENTS:

- 2 cups of spinach
- 1 cup of kale
- 1 green apple
- 1/2 cucumber
- 1/2 lime
- 1 tbsp chia seeds
- 1 cup of coconut water

INSTRUCTIONS:

1. Thoroughly clean all the components.

2. Slice the lime, cucumber, and green apple.

3. Blend the spinach, kale, green apple, cucumber, lime juice, chia seeds, and coconut water in a food processor.

4. Up to smooth, blend.

5. Pour into glasses, then offer.

NUTRITION INFO (PER SERVING):

Cals: 110

Fat: 2g

Carbs: 22g

Fiber: 8g

Protein: 4g

257.BERRY BLISS

Time: 10 mins

Servings: 2

INGREDIENTS:

- 1 cup of combined berries (strawberries, blueberries, raspberries)
- 1 banana
- 1 cup of almond milk
- 1 tbsp honey
- 1 tbsp flaxseeds (non-compulsory)

INSTRUCTIONS:

1. Thoroughly wash the berries.

2. The banana Must be peel off and chop-up.

3. Blend the combined berries, banana chunks, almond milk, honey, and flaxseeds (if using) together in a blender.

4. Up to smooth, blend.

5. Offer cold.

NUTRITION INFO (PER SERVING):

Cals: 130

Fat: 2g

Carbs: 30g

Fiber: 6g

Protein: 2g

258. CITRUS SPLASH

Time: 5 mins

Servings: 2

INGREDIENTS:

- 2 oranges
- 1 grapefruit
- 1 lemon
- 1 cup of cold water
- Ice cubes (non-compulsory)

INSTRUCTIONS:

1. Juice from oranges, grapefruit, and lemons Must be squeezed.

2. Citrus juices and cold water Must be mixd in a pitcher.

3. Stir thoroughly.

4. If desired, include ice cubes.

5. Offer cold.

NUTRITION INFO (PER SERVING):

Cals: 70

Fat: 0g

Carbs: 18g

Fiber: 4g

Protein: 1g

259.VEGGIE WONDER

Time: 10 mins

Servings: 2

INGREDIENTS:

- 2 carrots
- 2 celery stalks
- 1/2 beetroot
- 1/2 lemon
- 1 cup of water

INSTRUCTIONS:

1. Every veggie Must be properly washed.

2. Carrots and beets Must be peel off.

3. Beetroot, celery, and carrots Must all be chop-up up lightly.

4. Blend the carrot pieces, celery stalks, beetroot pieces, water, and lemon juice together in a blender.

5. Up to smooth, blend.

6. Offer cold.

NUTRITION INFO (PER SERVING):

Cals: 70

Fat: 0.5g

Carbs: 16g

Fiber: 4g

Protein: 2g

260.POWER POTION

Time: 10 mins

Servings: 2

INGREDIENTS:

- 2 cups of baby spinach
- 1 cup of kale
- 1/2 avocado
- 1 green apple
- 1 tbsp almond butter
- 1 cup of coconut water

INSTRUCTIONS:

1. Thoroughly clean all the components.

2. Slice the green apple and take off the core.

3. Baby spinach, kale, avocado, green apple slices, almond butter, and coconut water Must all be mixd in a blender.

4. Up to smooth, blend.

5. Offer cold.

NUTRITION INFO (PER SERVING):

Cals: 220

Fat: 10g

Carbs: 26g

Fiber: 9g

Protein: 8g

261.RAINBOW DELIGHT

Time: 10 mins

Servings: 2

INGREDIENTS:

- 1/2 cup of strawberries
- 1/2 cup of mango chunks
- 1/2 cup of pineapple chunks
- 1/2 cup of kiwi slices
- 1/2 cup of blueberries
- 1/2 cup of almond milk
- 1 tbsp honey
- 1 tbsp shredded coconut (non-compulsory)

INSTRUCTIONS:

1. Thoroughly wash every fruit.

2. Mango, pineapple, kiwi, strawberries, and other fruits Must all be chop-up up.

3. Strawberries, mango, pineapple, kiwi, blueberries, almond milk, and honey Must all be mixd in a blender.

4. Up to smooth, blend.

5. If preferred, top with coconut shreds.

6. Offer cold.

NUTRITION INFO (PER SERVING):

Cals: 140

Fat: 2g

Carbs: 34g

Fiber: 6g

Protein: 2g

262.LEMON LIME DELIGHT

Time: 5 mins

Servings: 2

INGREDIENTS:

- 2 lemons
- 2 limes
- 2 cups of water
- 2 tbsp honey
- Ice cubes (non-compulsory)
- Lemon and lime slices (for garnish)

INSTRUCTIONS:

1. Lemon and lime juice Must be squeezed.

2. Mix the lemon juice, lime juice, water, and honey in a pitcher.

3. Up to the honey is dissolved, stir thoroughly.

4. If desired, include ice cubes.

5. Slices of lime and lemon may be garnished.

6. Offer cold.

NUTRITION INFO (PER SERVING):

Cals: 60

Fat: 0g

Carbs: 18g

Fiber: 2g

Protein: 0g

263.ORANGE ZEST

Time: 5 mins

Servings: 2

INGREDIENTS:

- 3 oranges
- 1 tsp orange zest
- 1 cup of water
- 2 tbsp agave syrup or honey
- Ice cubes (non-compulsory)
- Orange slices (for garnish)

INSTRUCTIONS:

1. Orange juice Must be squeezed.

2. Orange juice, orange zest, water, and agave syrup or honey Must all be mixd in a pitcher.

3. Once the sweetener has dissolved, thoroughly stir.

4. If desired, include ice cubes.

5. Orange slices are a nice garnish.

6. Offer cold.

NUTRITION INFO (PER SERVING):

Cals: 80

Fat: 0g

Carbs: 20g

Fiber: 2g

Protein: 1g

264.CARROT KICK

Time: 10 mins

Servings: 2

INGREDIENTS:

- 2 Big carrots
- 1 orange
- 1/2 inch fresh ginger
- 1 tbsp lemon juice
- 1 cup of water
- Ice cubes (non-compulsory)
- Fresh mint leaves (for garnish)

INSTRUCTIONS:

1. Peel and wash the carrots.

2. Take out the orange's seeds after peeling it.

3. Slice the ginger, orange, and carrots lightly.

4. The diced carrots, orange pieces, ginger, lemon juice, and water Must all be put in a blender.

5. Up to smooth, blend.

6. If desired, include ice cubes.

7. Use fresh mint leaves as a garnish.

8. Offer cold.

NUTRITION INFO (PER SERVING):

Cals: 70

Fat: 0g

Carbs: 18g

Fiber: 4g

Protein: 2g

265.BEETROOT BLAST:

Time: 10 mins

Servings: 2

INGREDIENTS:

- 2 medium beetroots, peel off and chop-up
- 1 cup of pineapple chunks
- 1 mini banana
- 1 cup of coconut water

INSTRUCTIONS:

1. Blend the items together in a blender.
2. Blend till creamy and smooth.
3. Pour into glasses, then offer.

266.PINEAPPLE DELIGHT:

Time: 5 mins

Servings: 1

INGREDIENTS:

- 1 cup of pineapple chunks
- 1/2 cup of coconut milk
- 1/2 cup of ice cubes
- 1 tbsp honey (non-compulsory)

INSTRUCTIONS:

1. Pineapple pieces, coconut milk, ice cubes, and honey Must all be blended together.
2. Blend till creamy and smooth.

3. Place in a glass and sip.

267.MANGO MADNESS:

Time: 5 mins

Servings: 1

INGREDIENTS:

- 1 ripe mango, peel off and diced
- 1/2 cup of orange juice
- 1/2 cup of yogurt
- 1/2 cup of ice cubes

INSTRUCTIONS:

1. Blend the mango cubes, yogurt, orange juice, and ice cubes together in a blender.
2. Blend till creamy and smooth.
3. Pour cold liquid into a glass and serve.

268.WATERMELON WONDER:

Time: 5 mins

Servings: 2

INGREDIENTS:

- 2 cups of diced watermelon
- 1/2 cup of coconut water
- 1 tbsp lime juice
- Mint leaves for garnish (non-compulsory)

INSTRUCTIONS:

1. Coconut water, lime juice, and chop-up watermelon Must all be mixd in a blender.
2. Up to smooth, blend.
3. Pour into glasses, add some mint leaves as a garnish if you like, and then serve.

269. GINGER CRUSH:

Time: 10 mins

Servings: 1

INGREDIENTS:

- 1 inch ginger root, peel off and finely grated
- 1/2 cup of pineapple chunks
- 1 mini apple, cored and diced
- 1 cup of coconut water
- 1/2 cup of ice cubes

INSTRUCTIONS:

1. Blender ingredients: ginger, apple, pineapple pieces, coconut water, and ice cubes.
2. Blend everything thoroughly up to it's smooth.
3. Place in a glass and sip.

270. POMEGRANATE PASSION:

Time: 5 mins

Servings: 1

INGREDIENTS:

- 1 cup of pomegranate seeds
- 1/2 cup of orange juice
- 1 tbsp honey (non-compulsory)
- 1/2 cup of ice cubes

INSTRUCTIONS:

1. Blend ice cubes, orange juice, honey, and pomegranate seeds in a blender.
2. Blend up to foamy and well-mixd.
3. Pour cold liquid into a glass and serve.

271. BLUEBERRY BREEZE:

Time: 5 mins

Servings: 1

INGREDIENTS:

- 1 cup of blueberries
- 1/2 cup of almond milk
- 1/2 cup of yogurt
- 1 tbsp honey (non-compulsory)
- 1/2 cup of ice cubes

INSTRUCTIONS:

1. In a blender, mix blueberries, almond milk, yogurt, honey, and ice cubes.
2. Blend till creamy and smooth.
3. Place in a glass and sip.

272. RASPBERRY REFRESH:

Time: 5 mins

Servings: 1

INGREDIENTS:

- 1 cup of raspberries
- 1/2 cup of coconut water
- 1/2 cup of orange juice
- 1 tbsp honey (non-compulsory)
- 1/2 cup of ice cubes

INSTRUCTIONS:

1. Blend raspberries with ice cubes, coconut water, orange juice, honey, and other ingredients.
2. Blend everything thoroughly and smoothly.
3. Pour cold liquid into a glass and serve.

273. CREAMY DREAM:

Time: 5 mins

Servings: 1

INGREDIENTS:

- 1 ripe banana
- 1/2 cup of almond milk
- 1/4 cup of Greek yogurt
- 1 tbsp almond butter
- 1 tbsp honey (non-compulsory)
- 1/2 cup of ice cubes

INSTRUCTIONS:

1. Ripe banana, almond milk, Greek yogurt, almond butter, honey, and ice cubes Must all be mixd in a blender.
2. Blend up to smooth and creamy.
3. Place in a glass and sip.

274. KIWI SPARKLE:

Time: 5 mins

Servings: 1

INGREDIENTS:

- 2 ripe kiwis, peel off and diced
- 1/2 cup of apple juice
- 1/2 cup of sparkling water
- 1/2 cup of ice cubes

INSTRUCTIONS:

1. Blend together kiwis that have been diced, apple juice, sparkling water, and ice cubes.
2. Blend everything thoroughly up to it's smooth.
3. Pour cold liquid into a glass and serve.

275. PEAR PLEASER:

Time: 10 mins

Servings: 2

INGREDIENTS:

- 2 ripe pears, peel off and diced
- 1 cup of spinach leaves
- 1/2 cup of almond milk
- 1 tbsp honey
- 1/2 tsp vanilla extract

INSTRUCTIONS:

1. Blend the items together in a blender.
2. Blend till creamy and smooth.
3. Pour cold liquid into glasses and serve.

276. PEVERYY PUNCH:

Time: 15 mins

Servings: 4

INGREDIENTS:

- 2 ripe peveryes, pitted and split
- 1 cup of orange juice
- 1/2 cup of pineapple juice
- 1/4 cup of lemon juice
- 2 cups of sparkling water
- Ice cubes

INSTRUCTIONS:

1. The peveryes, orange juice, pineapple juice, and lemon juice Must all be thoroughly blended in a blender.
2. Fill a pitcher with the ingredients.
3. Gently stir in the sparkling water.

4. Over ice cubes, please.

277.STRAWBERRY SURPRISE:

Time: 5 mins

Servings: 1

INGREDIENTS:

- 1 cup of strawberries, hulled
- 1/2 cup of Greek yogurt
- 1/4 cup of almond milk
- 1 tbsp honey
- 1/2 tsp lemon zest

INSTRUCTIONS:

1. Blend the items together in a blender.
2. Blend till creamy and smooth.
3. Pour into a glass, then sip.

278.MELON MAGIC:

Time: 10 mins

Servings: 2

INGREDIENTS:

- 2 cups of diced watermelon
- 1 cup of diced cantaloupe
- 1 cup of diced honeydew melon
- Juice of 1 lime
- Mint leaves for garnish (non-compulsory)

INSTRUCTIONS:

1. Blend the honeydew, cantaloupe, and watermelon together in a blender.
2. juice of the lime; add.
3. Up to smooth, blend.

4. Pour into glasses and, if preferred, top with mint leaves.

279.GOLDEN GLOW:

Time: 5 mins

Servings: 1

INGREDIENTS:

- 1 Big carrot, peel off and chop-up
- 1 orange, peel off and segmented
- 1/2 inch fresh ginger, peel off
- 1/2 cup of coconut water
- Ice cubes

INSTRUCTIONS:

1. Blend the carrot, ginger, orange segments, and coconut water in a food processor.
2. Up to smooth, blend.
3. When the mixture is cold, add ice cubes and mix again.
4. To serve, pour into a glass.

180.MINTY COOL:

Time: 5 mins

Servings: 1

INGREDIENTS:

- 1 cup of fresh mint leaves
- 1/2 cup of cucumber, peel off and chop-up
- 1/2 cup of pineapple chunks
- 1/2 cup of coconut water
- 1 tbsp lime juice
- Ice cubes

INSTRUCTIONS:

1. Blend the items together in a blender.

2. Blend everything thoroughly up to it's smooth.
3. When the mixture is cold, add ice cubes and mix again.
4. Pour into a glass, then sip.

281.GREEN ENERGY:

Time: 5 mins

Servings: 1

INGREDIENTS:

- 1 cup of spinach leaves
- 1/2 avocado, pitted and peel off
- 1 green apple, cored and chop-up
- 1 cup of almond milk
- 1 tbsp honey
- Ice cubes

INSTRUCTIONS:

1. Blend the items together in a blender.
2. Blend till creamy and smooth.
3. When the mixture is cold, add ice cubes and mix again.
4. To serve, pour into a glass.

282.BERRY BURST:

Time: 10 mins

Servings: 2

INGREDIENTS:

- 1 cup of combined berries (strawberries, blueberries, raspberries)
- 1 banana
- 1 cup of Greek yogurt
- 1 cup of almond milk
- 1 tbsp honey
- Ice cubes

1. Blend the items together in a blender.
2. Blend till creamy and smooth.
3. When the mixture is cold, add ice cubes and mix again.
4. Pour into cups of, then sip.

283.CITRUS BLAST:

Time: 5 mins

Servings: 1

INGREDIENTS:

- Juice of 1 grapefruit
- Juice of 1 orange
- Juice of 1 lemon
- 1 tbsp honey
- Ice cubes

INSTRUCTIONS:

1. Mix the grapefruit juice, orange juice, lemon juice, and honey in a glass.
2. Up to the honey is dissolved, stir thoroughly.
3. Re-stir, then add the ice cubes.
4. Serve the zingy citrus explosion and enjoy it!

284.VEGGIE INFUSION:

Time: 10 mins

Servings: 2

INGREDIENTS:

- 1 cucumber, peel off and chop-up
- 2 celery stalks, chop-up
- 2 carrots, peel off and chop-up
- 1/2 lemon, juiced
- 1 cup of water

- Ice cubes

INSTRUCTIONS:

1. Blend the items together in a blender.
2. Up to smooth, blend.
3. When the mixture is cold, add ice cubes and mix again.
4. Pour into glasses, then savor the delicious veggie-infused beverage!

285.POWER PUNCH

Time: 5 mins

Servings: 2

INGREDIENTS:

- 1 cup of spinach leaves
- 1 medium banana
- 1/2 cup of Greek yogurt
- 1 tbsp almond butter
- 1 cup of almond milk
- 1 tbsp honey
- 1 tsp chia seeds

INSTRUCTIONS:

1. To a blender, add all the ingredients.

2. Blend till creamy and smooth.

3. Pour cold liquid into glasses and serve.

NUTRITION INFO PER SERVING:

Cals: 250

Protein: 10g

Fat: 8g

Carbs: 38g

Fiber: 6g

286.RAINBOW BLEND

Time: 10 mins

Servings: 4

INGREDIENTS:

- 1 cup of strawberries
- 1/2 cup of pineapple chunks
- 1/2 cup of mango chunks
- 1 medium carrot, peel off and chop-up
- 1/2 cup of orange juice
- 1/2 cup of coconut water
- 1 tbsp honey

INSTRUCTIONS:

1. Blend the items together in a blender.

2. Blend everything thoroughly up to it's smooth.

3. Pour into cups of, then sip.

NUTRITION INFO PER SERVING:

Cals: 120

Protein: 2g

Fat: 0.5g

Carbs: 29g

Fiber: 4g

287.LEMONADE FIZZ

Time: 5 mins

Servings: 2

INGREDIENTS:

- 2 lemons, juiced
- 1 lime, juiced
- 2 cups of sparkling water
- 2 tbsp honey
- Fresh mint leaves (for garnish)

INSTRUCTIONS:

1. Lemon juice, lime juice, sparkling water, and honey Must all be mixd in a pitcher.

2. Up to the honey is dissolved, stir thoroughly.

3. The lemonade fizz Must be poured into ice-filled glasses.

4. Serve cold and garnish with fresh mint leaves.

NUTRITION INFO PER SERVING:

Cals: 60

Protein: 0g

Fat: 0g

Carbs: 17g

Fiber: 1g

288.ORANGE CRUSH

Time: 5 mins

Servings: 2

INGREDIENTS:

- 2 oranges, peel off and segmented
- 1 cup of coconut water
- 1/2 cup of ice cubes
- 1 tbsp agave syrup or honey (non-compulsory)

INSTRUCTIONS:

1. Blend together the orange segments, coconut water, ice cubes, and honey or agave syrup (if using).

2. Blend up to foamy and well-mixd.

3. Pour cold liquid into glasses and serve.

NUTRITION INFO PER SERVING:

Cals: 80

Protein: 1g

Fat: 0g

Carbs: 20g

Fiber: 4g

289.CARROT CRAZE

Time: 5 mins

Servings: 2

INGREDIENTS:

- 2 Big carrots, peel off and chop-up
- 1 apple, cored and chop-up
- 1/2 cup of orange juice
- 1/2 cup of almond milk
- 1 tbsp fresh ginger, finely grated
- 1 tbsp lemon juice
- 1 tsp honey (non-compulsory)

INSTRUCTIONS:

1. In a blender, mix all the ingredients.

2. Blend till creamy and smooth.

3. If desired, taste and add honey.

4. Pour into glasses and start serving right away.

NUTRITION INFO PER SERVING:

Cals: 100

Protein: 2g

Fat: 1g

Carbs: 24g

Fiber: 4g

290.BEETROOT BEAUTY

Time: 10 mins

Servings: 2

INGREDIENTS:

- 1 medium beetroot, peel off and chop-up
- 1 cup of combined berries (strawberries, raspberries, blueberries)
- 1 cup of coconut water
- 1 tbsp honey
- 1/2 cup of ice cubes
- Fresh mint leaves (for garnish)

INSTRUCTIONS:

1. Blend the coconut water, honey, combined berries, beetroot, and ice cubes in a blender.

2. Blend everything thoroughly up to it's smooth.

3. Pour into glasses and top with mint leaves just picked.

4. Offer cold.

NUTRITION INFO PER SERVING:

Cals: 120

Protein: 2g

Fat: 1g

Carbs: 28g

Fiber: 6g

291.PINEAPPLE PARADISE

Time: 5 mins

Servings: 2

INGREDIENTS:

- 2 cups of fresh pineapple chunks
- 1 cup of coconut milk
- 1/2 cup of ice cubes
- 1 tbsp lime juice
- 1 tbsp honey (non-compulsory)
- Pineapple wedges (for garnish)

INSTRUCTIONS:

1. The pineapple chunks, coconut milk, ice cubes, lime juice, and honey (if used) Must all be blended together.

2. Blend till creamy and smooth.

3. Pour into glasses and add pineapple wedges as a garnish.

4. Offer cold.

NUTRITION INFO PER SERVING:

Cals: 150

Protein: 1g

Fat: 6g

Carbs: 25g

Fiber: 3g

292.MANGO MANIA

Time: 5 mins

Servings: 2

INGREDIENTS:

- 1 Big mango, peel off and chop-up
- 1 cup of coconut water
- 1/2 cup of plain Greek yogurt
- 1 tbsp honey
- 1/2 tsp vanilla extract
- 1/2 cup of ice cubes

INSTRUCTIONS:

1. In a blender, mix the mango, coconut water, honey, Greek yogurt, vanilla essence, and ice cubes.

2. Blend till creamy and smooth.

3. Pour cold liquid into glasses and serve.

NUTRITION INFO PER SERVING:

Cals: 180

Protein: 7g

Fat: 1g

Carbs: 39g

Fiber: 3g

293.WATERMELON SPLASH

Time: 5 mins

Servings: 2

INGREDIENTS:

- 2 cups of watermelon chunks
- 1/2 cup of fresh mint leaves
- 1 tbsp lime juice
- 1 tbsp honey (non-compulsory)
- 1/2 cup of ice cubes

INSTRUCTIONS:

1. Blend the watermelon pieces with the lime juice, mint leaves, ice cubes, and honey (if using).

2. Blend everything thoroughly up to it's smooth.

3. Pour cold liquid into glasses and serve.

NUTRITION INFO PER SERVING:

Cals: 80

Protein: 1g

Fat: 0g

Carbs: 21g

Fiber: 1g

294.GINGER ZING

Time: 5 mins

Servings: 2

INGREDIENTS:

- 1 mini apple, cored and chop-up
- 1/2 cup of cucumber, chop-up
- 1 tbsp fresh ginger, finely grated
- 1 tbsp lemon juice
- 1 cup of coconut water
- 1/2 cup of ice cubes
- Fresh mint leaves (for garnish)

INSTRUCTIONS:

1. Blend together the coconut water, apple, cucumber, ginger, lemon juice, and ice cubes.

2. Blend everything thoroughly up to it's smooth.

3. Pour into glasses and top with mint leaves just picked.

4. Offer cold.

NUTRITION INFO PER SERVING:

Cals: 70

Protein: 1g

Fat: 0g

Carbs: 18g

Fiber: 3g

295.POMEGRANATE POWER

Time: 5 mins

Servings: 2

INGREDIENTS:

- 1 cup of pomegranate seeds
- 1 cup of almond milk
- 1 banana
- 1 tbsp honey
- 1/2 cup of Greek yogurt
- 1 cup of ice cubes

INSTRUCTIONS:

1. Blend the items together in a blender.

2. Blend till creamy and smooth.

3. Pour into glasses and start serving right away.

NUTRITION INFO (PER SERVING):

Cals: 180

Protein: 6g

Fat: 3g

Carbs: 35g

Fiber: 5g

296.BLUEBERRY BLISS

Time: 5 mins

Servings: 2

INGREDIENTS:

- 1 cup of blueberries
- 1 cup of unsweetened coconut milk
- 1/2 cup of plain Greek yogurt
- 1 tbsp honey
- 1/2 tsp vanilla extract
- 1 cup of ice cubes

INSTRUCTIONS:

1. In a blender, mix all the ingredients.

2. Blend till creamy and smooth.

3. Pour into glasses and start serving right away.

NUTRITION INFO (PER SERVING):

Cals: 150

Protein: 5g

Fat: 4g

Carbs: 25g

Fiber: 4g

297.RASPBERRY REVIVE

Time: 5 mins

Servings: 2

INGREDIENTS:

- 1 cup of raspberries
- 1 cup of almond milk
- 1/2 cup of vanilla Greek yogurt
- 1 tbsp honey
- 1 tbsp chia seeds
- 1 cup of ice cubes

INSTRUCTIONS:

1. To a blender, add all the ingredients.

2. Blend everything thoroughly up to it's smooth.

3. Pour into glasses and start serving right away.

NUTRITION INFO (PER SERVING):

Cals: 180

Protein: 6g

Fat: 4g

Carbs: 30g

Fiber: 8g

298.CREAMY SUNSHINE

Time: 5 mins

Servings: 2

INGREDIENTS:

- 1 Big ripe mango
- 1 banana
- 1 cup of orange juice
- 1/2 cup of Greek yogurt
- 1 tbsp honey
- 1 cup of ice cubes

INSTRUCTIONS:

1. Mango and banana are peel off and chop-up.

2. Blend the items together in a blender.

3. Blend till creamy and smooth.

4. Pour into glasses and start serving right away.

NUTRITION INFO (PER SERVING):

Cals: 210

Protein: 5g

Fat: 1g

Carbs: 50g

Fiber: 4g

299.KIWI CRUSH

Time: 5 mins

Servings: 2

INGREDIENTS:

- 2 ripe kiwis
- 1 cup of spinach
- 1 cup of pineapple chunks
- 1/2 cup of coconut water
- 1 tbsp lime juice
- 1 cup of ice cubes

INSTRUCTIONS:

1. Slice and peel the kiwis.

2. Blend the items together in a blender.

3. Blend everything thoroughly up to it's smooth.

4. Pour into glasses and start serving right away.

NUTRITION INFO (PER SERVING):

Cals: 120

Protein: 2g

Fat: 1g

Carbs: 30g

Fiber: 6g

300.PEAR PLEASURE

Time: 5 mins

Servings: 2

INGREDIENTS:

- 2 ripe pears
- 1 cup of spinach
- 1 cup of unsweetened almond milk
- 1 tbsp honey
- 1 tbsp almond butter
- 1 cup of ice cubes

INSTRUCTIONS:

1. Pears must be peel off and cored.

2. Blend the items together in a blender.

3. Blend till creamy and smooth.

4. Pour into glasses and start serving right away.

NUTRITION INFO (PER SERVING):

Cals: 180

Protein: 4g

Fat: 4g

Carbs: 35g

Fiber: 8g

301.PEVERYY PARADISE

Time: 5 mins

Servings: 2

INGREDIENTS:

- 2 ripe peveryes
- 1 cup of coconut milk
- 1/2 cup of plain Greek yogurt
- 1 tbsp honey
- 1/2 tsp vanilla extract
- 1 cup of ice cubes

INSTRUCTIONS:

1. Slice and peel the peveryes.

2. Blend the items together in a blender.

3. Blend everything thoroughly up to it's smooth.

4. Pour into glasses and start serving right away.

NUTRITION INFO (PER SERVING):

Cals: 180

Protein: 6g

Fat: 4g

Carbs: 30g

Fiber: 3g

302.STRAWBERRY SWIRL

Time: 5 mins

Servings: 2

INGREDIENTS:

- 1 cup of strawberries
- 1 cup of unsweetened almond milk
- 1/2 cup of plain Greek yogurt
- 1 tbsp honey
- 1 tbsp flaxseed
- 1 cup of ice cubes

INSTRUCTIONS:

1. To a blender, add all the ingredients.

2. Blend till creamy and smooth.

3. Pour into glasses and start serving right away.

NUTRITION INFO (PER SERVING):

Cals: 140

Protein: 6g

Fat: 3g

Carbs: 25g

Fiber: 6g

303. MELON MADNESS

Time: 5 mins

Servings: 2

INGREDIENTS:

- 2 cups of cubed watermelon
- 1 cup of cantaloupe chunks
- 1 cup of honeydew chunks
- 1/2 cup of coconut water
- 1 tbsp lime juice
- 1 cup of ice cubes

INSTRUCTIONS:

1. Blend the items together in a blender.

2. Blend everything thoroughly up to it's smooth.

3. Pour into glasses and start serving right away.

NUTRITION INFO (PER SERVING):

Cals: 120

Protein: 2g

Fat: 1g

Carbs: 30g

Fiber: 2g

304.GOLDEN GODDESS

Time: 5 mins

Servings: 2

INGREDIENTS:

- 1 ripe banana
- 1 cup of pineapple chunks
- 1 cup of mango chunks
- 1 cup of orange juice
- 1 tbsp turmeric powder
- 1 cup of ice cubes

INSTRUCTIONS:

1. Chop the banana after peeling it.

2. Blend the items together in a blender.

3. Blend till creamy and smooth.

4. Pour into glasses and start serving right away.

NUTRITION INFO (PER SERVING):

Cals: 220

Protein: 2g

Fat: 1g

Carbs: 55g

Fiber: 4g

305.MINTY FRESHNESS

Time: 5 mins

Servings: 1

INGREDIENTS:

- 1 cup of fresh mint leaves
- 1/2 cup of cucumber, split
- 1 lime, juiced
- 1 tbsp honey
- Ice cubes
- Water

INSTRUCTIONS:

1. Mint leaves, cucumber slices, lime juice, honey, and a few ice cubes Must all be put in a blender.

2. Up to smooth, blend.

3. To achieve the correct consistency, add water.

4. Add a mint sprig as a garnish after pouring into a glass. Offer cold.

NUTRITION INFO:

Cals: 45

Carbs: 12g

Fiber: 2g

Protein: 1g

Fat: 0g

306.GREEN POWER

Time: 10 mins

Servings: 2

INGREDIENTS:

- 2 cups of spinach
- 1/2 cup of kale
- 1 green apple, cored and chop-up
- 1 ripe banana
- 1 cup of almond milk
- 1 tbsp chia seeds (non-compulsory)
- Ice cubes

INSTRUCTIONS:

1. Blend spinach, kale, green apple, banana, almond milk, chia seeds (if used), and a few ice cubes together in a blender.

2. Blend till creamy and smooth.

3. Pour into glasses and start serving right away.

NUTRITION INFO:

Cals: 150

Carbs: 32g

Fiber: 7g

Protein: 4g

Fat: 2g

307.BERRY BONANZA

Time: 5 mins

Servings: 1

INGREDIENTS:

- 1 cup of combined berries (strawberries, blueberries, raspberries)
- 1/2 cup of plain yogurt
- 1/2 cup of almond milk
- 1 tbsp honey
- Ice cubes

INSTRUCTIONS:

1. Blend together combined berries, yogurt, almond milk, honey, and a few ice cubes in a blender.

2. Blend till creamy and smooth.

3. Pour cold liquid into a glass and serve.

NUTRITION INFO:

Cals: 180

Carbs: 30g

Fiber: 6g

Protein: 8g

Fat: 3g

308.CITRUS SYMPHONY

Time: 5 mins

Servings: 1

INGREDIENTS:

- 1 orange, peel off
- 1 grapefruit, peel off
- 1 lemon, juiced
- 1 tbsp agave syrup or honey
- Ice cubes

INSTRUCTIONS:

1. Orange, grapefruit, lemon juice, agave syrup (or honey), and a few ice cubes Must all be mixd in a blender.

2. Blend everything thoroughly up to it's smooth.

3. Pour cold liquid into a glass and serve.

NUTRITION INFO:

Cals: 100

Carbs: 24g

Fiber: 4g

Protein: 2g

Fat: 0g

309. VEGGIE VITALITY

Time: 10 mins

Servings: 2

INGREDIENTS:

- 2 Big carrots, peel off and chop-up
- 1 cucumber, chop-up
- 2 stalks celery, chop-up
- 1 green apple, cored and chop-up
- 1/2 lemon, juiced
- 1-inch piece of ginger, peel off
- Ice cubes

INSTRUCTIONS:

1. Green apple, cucumber, celery, carrots, lemon juice, ginger, and a few ice cubes Must all be added to a blender.

2. Blend everything thoroughly up to it's smooth.

3. Pour cold liquid into glasses and serve.

NUTRITION INFO:

Cals: 110

Carbs: 26g

Fiber: 6g

Protein: 2g

Fat: 1g

310.POWER FUEL

Time: 5 mins

Servings: 1

INGREDIENTS:

- 1 banana
- 1/2 cup of cooked quinoa
- 1 tbsp almond butter
- 1 cup of almond milk
- 1 tbsp honey
- Ice cubes

INSTRUCTIONS:

1. Banana, cooked quinoa, almond butter, almond milk, honey, and a few ice cubes Must all be mixd in a blender.

2. Blend till creamy and smooth.

3. Pour cold liquid into a glass and serve.

NUTRITION INFO:

Cals: 350

Carbs: 61g

Fiber: 8g

Protein: 10g

Fat: 9g

311.RAINBOW REFRESHER

Time: 5 mins

Servings: 1

INGREDIENTS:

- 1/2 cup of chop-up pineapple
- 1/2 cup of chop-up watermelon
- 1/2 cup of chop-up mango
- 1/2 cup of chop-up papaya
- 1/2 cup of coconut water
- Ice cubes

INSTRUCTIONS:

1. Chop up pineapple, watermelon, mango, papaya, coconut water, and a few ice cubes, and put in a blender.

2. Blend everything thoroughly up to it's smooth.

3. Pour cold liquid into a glass and serve.

NUTRITION INFO:

Cals: 160

Carbs: 40g

Fiber: 4g

Protein: 2g

Fat: 1g

312. LEMON LIME FIZZ

Time: 5 mins

Servings: 1

INGREDIENTS:

- Juice of 1 lemon
- Juice of 1 lime
- 1 tbsp agave syrup or honey
- Sparkling water
- Ice cubes

INSTRUCTIONS:

1. Lemon juice, lime juice, and agave syrup (or honey) Must all be mixd in a glass. Stir thoroughly.

2. A few ice cubes are placed in the glass after the sparkling water has been added.

3. Gently stir, then serve cold.

NUTRITION INFO:

Cals: 40

Carbs: 12g

Fiber: 0g

Protein: 0g

Fat: 0g

313.ORANGE OASIS

Time: 5 mins

Servings: 1

INGREDIENTS:

- 2 oranges, peel off
- 1 carrot, peel off and chop-up
- 1/2 inch fresh ginger, peel off
- 1 tbsp honey
- Ice cubes

INSTRUCTIONS:

1. Peel off oranges, diced carrot, ginger, honey, and a few ice cubes Must all be put in a blender.

2. Blend everything thoroughly up to it's smooth.

3. Pour cold liquid into a glass and serve.

NUTRITION INFO:

Cals: 120

Carbs: 28g

Fiber: 4g

Protein: 2g

Fat: 0g

314. CARROT CRUNCH

Time: 5 mins

Servings: 1

INGREDIENTS:

- 2 Big carrots, peel off and chop-up
- 1 apple, cored and chop-up
- 1/2 inch fresh ginger, peel off
- 1 tbsp lemon juice
- Ice cubes

INSTRUCTIONS:

1. Chop-up carrots, apple, ginger, lemon juice, and a few ice cubes Must all be put in a blender.

2. Blend everything thoroughly up to it's smooth.

3. Pour cold liquid into a glass and serve.

NUTRITION INFO:

Cals: 90

Carbs: 22g

Fiber: 4g

Protein: 1g

Fat: 0g

315.BEETROOT BLAST

Time: 10 mins

Servings: 2

INGREDIENTS:

- 2 medium-sized beetroots, peel off and chop-up
- 1 cup of refrigerate strawberries
- 1 ripe banana
- 1 cup of almond milk
- 1 tbsp honey (non-compulsory)

INSTRUCTIONS:

1. Blend the items together in a blender.

2. Blend till creamy and smooth.

3. Taste, and if necessary, add honey to balance sweetness.

4. Pour into glasses and start serving right away.

NUTRITION INFO (PER SERVING):

Cals: 150

Fat: 1g

Carbs: 35g

Fiber: 5g

Protein: 3g

316. PINEAPPLE PARTY

Time: 5 mins

Servings: 1

INGREDIENTS:

- 1 cup of refrigerate pineapple chunks
- 1/2 cup of coconut milk
- 1/4 cup of orange juice
- 1/2 tsp vanilla extract

INSTRUCTIONS:

1. Mix all the ingredients in a blender.

2. Blend till creamy and smooth.

3. Pour into a glass, then serve right away.

NUTRITION INFO (PER SERVING):

Cals: 180

Fat: 8g

Carbs: 25g

Fiber: 2g

Protein: 1g

317.MANGO MAGIC

Time: 5 mins

Servings: 2

INGREDIENTS:

- 2 ripe mangoes, peel off and pitted
- 1 cup of plain yogurt
- 1/2 cup of orange juice
- 1 tbsp honey (non-compulsory)

INSTRUCTIONS:

1. Blend the items together in a blender.

2. Blend till creamy and smooth.

3. If more sweetness is wanted, taste and add honey.

4. Pour into glasses and start serving right away.

NUTRITION INFO (PER SERVING):

Cals: 200

Fat: 2g

Carbs: 45g

Fiber: 4g

Protein: 6g

318.WATERMELON WAVE

Time: 5 mins

Servings: 2

INGREDIENTS:

- 2 cups of cubed watermelon, seeds take outd
- 1 cup of fresh strawberries
- 1/2 cup of coconut water
- Juice of 1 lime
- 1 tbsp agave syrup (non-compulsory)

INSTRUCTIONS:

1. Blend the items together in a blender.

2. Blend everything thoroughly up to it's smooth.

3. If more sweetness is wanted, taste and add agave nectar.

4. Pour into glasses and start serving right away.

NUTRITION INFO (PER SERVING):

Cals: 80

Fat: 0g

Carbs: 20g

Fiber: 2g

Protein: 1g

319.GINGER SNAP

Time: 7 mins

Servings: 1

INGREDIENTS:

- 1 cup of fresh pineapple chunks
- 1 mini apple, cored and chop-up
- 1/2-inch piece of fresh ginger, peel off and finely grated
- 1/2 cup of coconut water
- 1 tbsp lime juice
- 1 tsp honey (non-compulsory)

INSTRUCTIONS:

1. Mix all the ingredients in a blender.

2. Blend everything thoroughly up to it's smooth.

3. If more sweetness is wanted, taste and add honey.

4. Pour into a glass, then serve right away.

NUTRITION INFO (PER SERVING):

Cals: 150

Fat: 0g

Carbs: 40g

Fiber: 5g

Protein: 1g

320.POMEGRANATE PLEASURE

Time: 5 mins

Servings: 1

INGREDIENTS:

- 1 cup of pomegranate seeds
- 1/2 cup of Greek yogurt
- 1/4 cup of almond milk
- 1 tbsp honey (non-compulsory)

INSTRUCTIONS:

1. Blend the items together in a blender.

2. Blend till creamy and smooth.

3. If honey is preferred, taste it and add.

4. Pour into a glass, then serve right away.

NUTRITION INFO (PER SERVING):

Cals: 180

Fat: 3g

Carbs: 35g

Fiber: 5g

Protein: 9g

321.BLUEBERRY BLAST

Time: 5 mins

Servings: 2

INGREDIENTS:

- 2 cups of fresh or refrigerate blueberries
- 1 cup of almond milk
- 1 ripe banana
- 1 tbsp chia seeds
- 1 tbsp honey (non-compulsory)

INSTRUCTIONS:

1. Mix all the ingredients in a blender.

2. Blend everything thoroughly up to it's smooth.

3. If honey is preferred, taste it and add.

4. Pour into glasses and start serving right away.

NUTRITION INFO (PER SERVING):

Cals: 170

Fat: 3g

Carbs: 35g

Fiber: 8g

Protein: 3g

322.RASPBERRY RIPPLE

Time: 5 mins

Servings: 1

INGREDIENTS:

- 1 cup of fresh raspberries
- 1/2 cup of coconut milk
- 1/4 cup of plain yogurt
- 1 tbsp honey (non-compulsory)

INSTRUCTIONS:

1. Use a blender to mix all the items.

2. Blend till creamy and smooth.

3. If honey is preferred, taste it and add it.

4. Pour into a glass, then serve right away.

NUTRITION INFO (PER SERVING):

Cals: 120

Fat: 7g

Carbs: 15g

Fiber: 5g

Protein: 2g

323. CREAMSICLE CREAMINESS

Time: 5 mins

Servings: 2

INGREDIENTS:

- 2 ripe oranges, peel off and segmented
- 1 cup of plain Greek yogurt
- 1/2 cup of almond milk
- 1 tbsp honey (non-compulsory)

INSTRUCTIONS:

1. Mix all the ingredients in a blender.
2. Blend till creamy and smooth.
3. If honey is preferred, taste it and add.
4. Pour into glasses and start serving right away.

NUTRITION INFO (PER SERVING):

Cals: 150

Fat: 0g

Carbs: 25g

Fiber: 4g

Protein: 10g

324.KIWI KISS

Time: 5 mins

Servings: 2

INGREDIENTS:

- 2 ripe kiwis, peel off and split
- 1 cup of spinach
- 1/2 cup of coconut water
- Juice of 1 lime
- 1 tbsp honey (non-compulsory)

INSTRUCTIONS:

1. Blend the items together in a blender.

2. Blend everything thoroughly up to it's smooth.

3. If honey is preferred, taste it and add.

4. Pour into glasses and start serving right away.

NUTRITION INFO (PER SERVING):

Cals: 90

Fat: 0g

Carbs: 20g

Fiber: 5g

Protein: 2g

325.PEAR PLEASURE:

Time: 15 mins

Servings: 2

INGREDIENTS:

- 2 ripe pears
- 1 cup of plain yogurt
- 1 tbsp honey
- 1/4 cup of granola
- Fresh mint leaves (for garnish)

INSTRUCTIONS:

1. Pears Must be peel off and cored before being slice into slices.

2. Pears, yogurt, and honey Must all be mixd in a blender. Up to smooth, blend.

3. Put the mixture into dishes for dishing. Add granola on top, then add mint leaves as a decoration.

4. Offer cold.

NUTRITION INFO (PER SERVING):

Cals: 180

Protein: 5g

Fat: 3g

Carbs: 35g

Fiber: 5g

326.PEVERYY PASSION:

Time: 10 mins

Servings: 1

INGREDIENTS:

- 1 ripe pevery
- 1/2 cup of orange juice
- 1/4 cup of plain Greek yogurt
- 1 tbsp chia seeds
- 1 tsp agave syrup (non-compulsory)

INSTRUCTIONS:

1. The pevery Must be peel off, pitted, and then chop-up.

2. Blend the pevery, orange juice, Greek yogurt, chia seeds, and agave syrup (if using) together in a blender. Up to smooth, blend.

3. Serve the mixture immediately after pouring it into a glass.

NUTRITION INFO (PER SERVING):

Cals: 180

Protein: 9g

Fat: 4g

Carbs: 32g

Fiber: 8g

327.STRAWBERRY SWIRL:

Time: 5 mins

Servings: 1

INGREDIENTS:

- 1 cup of refrigerate strawberries
- 1/2 cup of almond milk
- 1 tbsp honey
- Fresh strawberries (for garnish)

1. Blend the refrigerate strawberries, almond milk, and honey together in a blender. Up to smooth, blend.

2. Put a glass with the mixture inside. Use fresh strawberries as a garnish.

3. Serve right away.

NUTRITION INFO (PER SERVING):

Cals: 120

Protein: 2g

Fat: 1g

Carbs: 28g

Fiber: 6g

328.MELON MEDLEY:

Time: 10 mins

Servings: 2

INGREDIENTS:

- 1 cup of diced watermelon
- 1 cup of diced cantaloupe
- 1 cup of diced honeydew melon
- 1 tbsp lime juice
- Fresh mint leaves (for garnish)

INSTRUCTIONS:

1. Mix the chop-up watermelon, cantaloupe, and honeydew melon in a big bowl.

2. Lime juice Must be drizzled over the melon, then gently combined in.

3. To serve, divide the melon mixture among bowls. Use fresh mint leaves as a garnish.

4. Offer cold.

NUTRITION INFO (PER SERVING):

Cals: 60

Protein: 1g

Fat: 0g

Carbs: 16g

Fiber: 2g

329.GOLDEN SUNSHINE:

Time: 5 mins

Servings: 1

INGREDIENTS:

- 1 Big ripe banana
- 1 cup of fresh orange juice
- 1/2 cup of pineapple chunks
- 1/4 cup of coconut milk

INSTRUCTIONS:

1. Blend the banana, orange juice, pineapple chunks, and coconut milk together in a blender. Up to smooth, blend.

2. Serve the mixture immediately after pouring it into a glass.

NUTRITION INFO (PER SERVING):

Cals: 230

Protein: 3g

Fat: 6g

Carbs: 47g

Fiber: 5g

330. MINT MOJITO:

Time: 5 mins

Servings: 1

INGREDIENTS:

- 1 cup of fresh lime juice
- 1/4 cup of fresh mint leaves
- 2 tbsp honey
- 1 cup of sparkling water
- Crushed ice

INSTRUCTIONS:

1. Mix the lime juice, mint leaves, and honey in a blender. Mint leaves Must be blended up to very lightly chop-up.

2. Crushed ice Must be added to a glass. Over the ice, pour the combined mixture.

3. Add sparkling water on top, then gently swirl.

4. Add a mint sprig as a garnish.

5. Serve right away.

NUTRITION INFO (PER SERVING):

Cals: 100

Protein: 1g

Fat: 0g

Carbs: 27g

Fiber: 1g

331.GREEN REVIVAL:

Time: 8 mins

Servings: 1

INGREDIENTS:

- 1 cup of spinach leaves
- 1 ripe banana
- 1/2 cup of cucumber slices
- 1/2 cup of green grapes
- 1/2 cup of almond milk

INSTRUCTIONS:

1. Blend the spinach leaves, banana, cucumber slices, green grapes, and almond milk in a food processor. Up to smooth, blend.

2. Serve the mixture immediately after pouring it into a glass.

NUTRITION INFO (PER SERVING):

Cals: 140

Protein: 3g

Fat: 2g

Carbs: 32g

Fiber: 4g

332.BERRY BOOST:

Time: 5 mins

Servings: 1

INGREDIENTS:

- 1 cup of combined berries (strawberries, blueberries, raspberries)
- 1/2 cup of plain yogurt
- 1/4 cup of almond milk
- 1 tbsp honey
- Fresh mint leaves (for garnish)

INSTRUCTIONS:

1. Blend the combined berries, plain yogurt, almond milk, and honey together in a blender. Up to smooth, blend.

2. Put a glass with the mixture inside. Use fresh mint leaves as a garnish.

3. Serve right away.

NUTRITION INFO (PER SERVING):

Cals: 150

Protein: 5g

Fat: 2g

Carbs: 30g

Fiber: 6g

333.CITRUS SYMPHONY:

Time: 10 mins

Servings: 2

INGREDIENTS:

- 2 oranges
- 1 grapefruit
- 1 lemon
- 1 tbsp honey
- Fresh mint leaves (for garnish)

INSTRUCTIONS:

1. Orange, grapefruit, and lemon juice Must be made.

2. The freshly squeezed citrus juices and honey Must be mixd in a pitcher. Stir thoroughly.

3. Place serving glasses with the mixture in them. Use fresh mint leaves as a garnish.

4. Offer cold.

NUTRITION INFO (PER SERVING):

Cals: 80

Protein: 1g

Fat: 0g

Carbs: 20g

Fiber: 3g

334. VEGGIE DELIGHT:

Time: 10 mins

Servings: 2

INGREDIENTS:

- 1 Big carrot
- 1/2 cucumber
- 1 stalk celery
- 1/2 green apple
- 1 cup of spinach leaves
- 1 cup of water
- 1 tbsp lemon juice

INSTRUCTIONS:

1. Chop the carrot after peeling it. Cucumbers are peel off and chop-up. Chop the green apple and celery.

2. The chop-up fruits and vegetables, spinach leaves, water, and lemon juice Must all be mixd in a blender. Up to smooth, blend.

3. Place serving glasses with the mixture in them. Offer cold.

NUTRITION INFO (PER SERVING):

Cals: 60

Protein: 2g

Fat: 0g

Carbs: 15g

Fiber: 4g

335.POWER POTION:

Time: 5 mins

Servings: 1

INGREDIENTS:

- 1 cup of spinach
- 1/2 cup of kale
- 1 banana
- 1/2 cup of almond milk
- 1 tbsp chia seeds
- 1 tsp honey

INSTRUCTIONS:

1. Blend spinach, kale, banana, almond milk, chia seeds, and honey in a blender.

2. Blend everything thoroughly up to it's smooth.

3. Place in a glass and sip.

NUTRITION INFO (PER SERVING):

Cals: 200

Protein: 6g

Fat: 5g

Carbs: 36g

Fiber: 8g

336.RAINBOW RIOT:

Time: 10 mins

Servings: 2

INGREDIENTS:

- 1 cup of refrigerate combined berries
- 1/2 cup of plain Greek yogurt
- 1/2 cup of orange juice
- 1/2 cup of coconut water
- 1 tbsp honey

INSTRUCTIONS:

1. Refrigerate combined berries, Greek yogurt, orange juice, coconut water, and honey Must all be blended together.

2. Blend till creamy and smooth.

3. Serve the mixture in two glasses.

NUTRITION INFO (PER SERVING):

Cals: 150

Protein: 6g

Fat: 1g

Carbs: 30g

Fiber: 4g

337.LEMON LIME FUSION:

Time: 5 mins

Servings: 1

INGREDIENTS:

- Juice of 1 lemon
- Juice of 1 lime
- 1 tbsp agave syrup
- 1 cup of sparkling water
- Ice cubes

INSTRUCTIONS:

1. Mix the agave syrup, lime juice, and lemon juice in a glass.

2. Agave syrup must be stirred up to it dissolves.

3. Pour sparkling water over the ice cubes.

4. Stir gently, then devour.

NUTRITION INFO (PER SERVING):

Cals: 50

Protein: 0g

Fat: 0g

Carbs: 15g

Fiber: 0g

338.ORANGE OASIS:

Time: 5 mins

Servings: 1

INGREDIENTS:

- 1 orange, peel off and segmented
- 1/2 cup of coconut water
- 1/4 cup of pineapple juice
- Ice cubes

INSTRUCTIONS:

1. Orange segments, coconut water, and pineapple juice Must all be mixd in a blender.

2. Up to smooth, blend.

3. Pour into a glass with ice cubes and serve.

NUTRITION INFO (PER SERVING):

Cals: 80

Protein: 1g

Fat: 0g

Carbs: 20g

Fiber: 3g

339.CARROT CRAZE:

Time: 8 mins

Servings: 2

INGREDIENTS:

- 2 Big carrots, peel off and chop-up
- 1 orange, peel off and segmented
- 1/2 cup of almond milk
- 1 tbsp honey
- Ice cubes

INSTRUCTIONS:

1. The diced carrots, orange segments, almond milk, and honey Must all be mixd in a blender.

2. Blend till creamy and smooth.

3. Serving cups of with ice cubes Must then be filled with the carrot combination.

4. Serve after a gentle stir.

NUTRITION INFO (PER SERVING):

Cals: 120

Protein: 2g

Fat: 1g

Carbs: 28g

Fiber: 4g

340. BEETROOT BLISS:

Time: 5 mins

Servings: 1

INGREDIENTS:

- 1 mini beetroot, peel off and chop-up
- 1 apple, cored and chop-up
- 1/2 cup of coconut water
- Juice of 1/2 lemon
- Ice cubes

INSTRUCTIONS:

1. The diced beetroot, apple, coconut water, and lemon juice Must all be mixd in a blender.

2. Up to smooth, blend.

3. Pour into a glass with ice cubes and serve.

NUTRITION INFO (PER SERVING):

Cals: 100

Protein: 1g

Fat: 0g

Carbs: 25g

Fiber: 4g

341.PINEAPPLE PARADISE:

Time: 5 mins

Servings: 1

INGREDIENTS:

- 1 cup of pineapple chunks
- 1/2 cup of coconut milk
- 1/4 cup of orange juice
- 1/4 tsp vanilla extract
- Ice cubes

INSTRUCTIONS:

1. The pineapple chunks, coconut milk, orange juice, and vanilla extract Must all be blended together.

2. Blend till creamy and smooth.

3. Pour into a glass with ice cubes and serve.

NUTRITION INFO (PER SERVING):

Cals: 150

Protein: 1g

Fat: 6g

Carbs: 25g

Fiber: 2g

342.MANGO MAGIC:

Time: 5 mins

Servings: 1

INGREDIENTS:

- 1 ripe mango, peel off and pitted
- 1/2 cup of plain yogurt
- 1/4 cup of orange juice
- Ice cubes

INSTRUCTIONS:

1. Blend the ripe mango, plain yogurt, and orange juice together in a blender.

2. Blend till creamy and smooth.

3. Pour into a glass with ice cubes and serve.

NUTRITION INFO (PER SERVING):

Cals: 180

Protein: 5g

Fat: 1g

Carbs: 40g

Fiber: 4g

343. WATERMELON WHIRL:

Time: 5 mins

Servings: 2

INGREDIENTS:

- 2 cups of diced watermelon
- 1/2 cup of fresh mint leaves
- Juice of 1 lime
- 1 tbsp honey
- Ice cubes

INSTRUCTIONS:

1. Watermelon diced, fresh mint leaves, lime juice, and honey Must all be mixd in a blender.

2. Up to smooth, blend.

3. Serving cups of Must first be filled with ice cubes before the watermelon mixture is added.

4. Serve after a gentle stir.

NUTRITION INFO (PER SERVING):

Cals: 80

Protein: 1g

Fat: 0g

Carbs: 20g

Fiber: 1g

344.GINGER SPICE:

Time: 7 mins

Servings: 1

INGREDIENTS:

- 1 tbsp freshly finely grated ginger
- 1 cup of water
- 1 tsp honey
- Juice of 1/2 lemon
- Ice cubes

INSTRUCTIONS:

1. Bring the finely grated ginger and water to a boil in a mini saucepan.

2. Turn down the heat, then simmer it for five mins.

3. Take out the ginger-infused water from the heat and pour it into a glass.

4. Add honey and lemon juice and stir.

5. Enjoy with ice cubes added.

NUTRITION INFO (PER SERVING):

Cals: 30

Protein: 0g

Fat: 0g

Carbs: 8g

Fiber: 0g

345.POMEGRANATE POTION:

Time: 5 mins

Servings: 2

INGREDIENTS:

- 1 cup of pomegranate seeds
- 1 cup of unsweetened almond milk
- 1 tbsp honey
- 1/2 tsp vanilla extract
- Ice cubes

INSTRUCTIONS:

1. Pomegranate seeds, almond milk, honey, and vanilla extract Must all be blended together.

2. Up to smooth, blend.

3. Blend again while adding ice cubes up to thoroughly blended.

4. Pour cold liquid into glasses and serve.

NUTRITION INFO (PER SERVING):

Cals: 120

Fat: 3g

Carbs: 24g

Protein: 1g

346.BLUEBERRY BURST:

Time: 7 mins

Servings: 2

INGREDIENTS:

- 1 cup of blueberries
- 1/2 cup of plain Greek yogurt
- 1/2 cup of almond milk
- 1 tbsp honey
- 1/2 tsp lemon zest
- Ice cubes

INSTRUCTIONS:

1. Blend blueberries, Greek yogurt, almond milk, honey, and lemon zest in a food processor.

2. Up to smooth, blend.

3. Blend again while adding ice cubes up to thoroughly blended.

4. Pour cold liquid into glasses and serve.

NUTRITION INFO (PER SERVING):

Cals: 130

Fat: 2g

Carbs: 24g

Protein: 7g

347.RASPBERRY RHAPSODY:

Time: 6 mins

Servings: 2

INGREDIENTS:

- 1 cup of raspberries
- 1 cup of coconut milk
- 1 tbsp maple syrup
- 1/2 tsp lime juice
- Ice cubes

INSTRUCTIONS:

1. Raspberries, coconut milk, maple syrup, and lime juice are all mixd in a blender.

2. Up to smooth, blend.

3. Blend again while adding ice cubes up to thoroughly blended.

4. Pour cold liquid into glasses and serve.

NUTRITION INFO (PER SERVING):

Cals: 150

Fat: 9g

Carbs: 18g

Protein: 2g

348.CREAMY CITRUS:

Time: 5 mins

Servings: 2

INGREDIENTS:

- 1 Big orange, peel off and segmented
- 1 Big grapefruit, peel off and segmented
- 1/2 cup of plain yogurt
- 1 tbsp honey
- Ice cubes

INSTRUCTIONS:

1. Blend orange and grapefruit segments, plain yogurt, and honey together in a blender.

2. Up to smooth, blend.

3. Blend again while adding ice cubes up to thoroughly blended.

4. Pour cold liquid into glasses and serve.

NUTRITION INFO (PER SERVING):

Cals: 120

Fat: 2g

Carbs: 24g

Protein: 5g

349.KIWI DELIGHT:

Time: 6 mins

Servings: 2

INGREDIENTS:

- 2 kiwis, peel off and split
- 1 banana
- 1/2 cup of spinach leaves
- 1/2 cup of coconut water
- 1 tbsp chia seeds
- Ice cubes

INSTRUCTIONS:

1. Blend spinach leaves, kiwis, bananas, coconut water, and chia seeds in a food processor.

2. Up to smooth, blend.

3. Blend again while adding ice cubes up to thoroughly blended.

4. Pour cold liquid into glasses and serve.

NUTRITION INFO (PER SERVING):

Cals: 160

Fat: 3g

Carbs: 32g

Protein: 5g

350. PEAR PARADISE:

Time: 5 mins

Servings: 2

INGREDIENTS:

- 2 ripe pears, cored and diced
- 1 cup of almond milk
- 1 tbsp honey
- 1/2 tsp cinnamon
- Ice cubes

INSTRUCTIONS:

1. Pears in dice, almond milk, honey, and cinnamon are mixd in a blender.

2. Up to smooth, blend.

3. Blend again while adding ice cubes up to thoroughly blended.

4. Pour cold liquid into glasses and serve.

NUTRITION INFO (PER SERVING):

Cals: 140

Fat: 2g

Carbs: 30g

Protein: 1g

351.PEVERY PERFECTION:

Time: 6 mins

Servings: 2

INGREDIENTS:

- 2 ripe peveryes, pitted and split
- 1/2 cup of vanilla Greek yogurt
- 1/2 cup of orange juice
- 1 tbsp agave syrup
- Ice cubes

INSTRUCTIONS:

1. Split peveryes, Greek yogurt, orange juice, and agave syrup Must all be mixd in a blender.

2. Up to smooth, blend.

3. Blend again while adding ice cubes up to thoroughly blended.

4. Pour cold liquid into glasses and serve.

NUTRITION INFO (PER SERVING):

Cals: 160

Fat: 2g

Carbs: 34g

Protein: 6g

352.STRAWBERRY SMOOTHIE:

Time: 5 mins

Servings: 2

INGREDIENTS:

- 1 cup of strawberries
- 1/2 cup of coconut milk
- 1/2 cup of plain Greek yogurt
- 1 tbsp honey
- Ice cubes

INSTRUCTIONS:

1. Strawberries, coconut milk, Greek yogurt, and honey are all mixd in a blender.

2. Up to smooth, blend.

3. Blend again while adding ice cubes up to thoroughly blended.

4. Pour cold liquid into glasses and serve.

NUTRITION INFO (PER SERVING):

Cals: 140

Fat: 4g

Carbs: 23g

Protein: 7g

353.MELON MANIA:

Time: 6 mins

Servings: 2

INGREDIENTS:

- 1 cup of cubed watermelon
- 1 cup of cubed cantaloupe
- 1/2 cup of cubed honeydew melon
- 1/2 cup of coconut water
- 1 tbsp lime juice
- Ice cubes

INSTRUCTIONS:

1. Blend watermelon, cantaloupe, honeydew melon, coconut water, and lime juice together in a blender.

2. Up to smooth, blend.

3. Blend again while adding ice cubes up to thoroughly blended.

4. Pour cold liquid into glasses and serve.

NUTRITION INFO (PER SERVING):

Cals: 90

Fat: 0g

Carbs: 22g

Protein: 2g

354.GOLDEN ELIXIR:

Time: 5 mins

Servings: 2

INGREDIENTS:

- 2 oranges, peel off and segmented
- 1 mini carrot, peel off and chop-up
- 1/2 inch fresh ginger, peel off
- 1/2 tsp turmeric powder
- 1/2 cup of coconut water
- Ice cubes

INSTRUCTIONS:

1. Orange segments, diced carrot, ginger, turmeric powder, and coconut water Must all be mixd in a blender.

2. Up to smooth, blend.

3. Blend again while adding ice cubes up to thoroughly blended.

4. Pour cold liquid into glasses and serve.

NUTRITION INFO (PER SERVING):

Cals: 110

Fat: 0g

Carbs: 26g

Protein: 2g

355. MINT MARVEL

Time: 10 mins

Servings: 2

INGREDIENTS:

- 2 cups of fresh mint leaves
- 2 cups of water
- 1 tbsp honey or sugar
- Ice cubes

INSTRUCTIONS:

1. Mint leaves, water, and honey or sugar Must all be blended together.

2. Blend everything thoroughly up to it's smooth.

3. Take out any particles from the mixture by straining.

4. Over ice cubes, please.

5. If desired, add mint leaves as a garnish.

NUTRITION (PER SERVING):

Cals: 25

Fat: 0g

Carbs: 6g

Fiber: 2g

Protein: 1g

356.GREEN GARDEN

Time: 15 mins

Servings: 4

INGREDIENTS:

- 2 cups of spinach leaves
- 1 cucumber, peel off and chop-up
- 1 green apple, cored and chop-up
- 1 celery stalk, chop-up
- 1 cup of water
- Juice of 1 lemon
- Ice cubes

INSTRUCTIONS:

1. Spinach leaves, cucumber, green apple, celery, water, and lemon juice Must all be mixd in a blender.
2. Blend everything thoroughly up to it's smooth.
3. Over ice cubes, please.

NUTRITION (PER SERVING):

Cals: 45

Fat: 0g

Carbs: 11g

Fiber: 3g

Protein: 1g

357.BERRY BOOST

Time: 5 mins

Servings: 2

INGREDIENTS:

- 1 cup of combined berries (strawberries, blueberries, raspberries)
- 1 cup of almond milk
- 1 tbsp honey or maple syrup
- Ice cubes

INSTRUCTIONS:

1. Blend the combined berries, almond milk, and honey or maple syrup together in a blender.

2. Blend everything thoroughly up to it's smooth.

3. Over ice cubes, please.

NUTRITION (PER SERVING):

Cals: 80

Fat: 2g

Carbs: 15g

Fiber: 4g

Protein: 1g

358.CITRUS DELIGHT

Time: 10 mins

Servings: 2

INGREDIENTS:

- 2 oranges, peel off and segmented
- 1 grapefruit, peel off and segmented
- 1 lime, juiced
- 1 tbsp honey or sugar
- Ice cubes

INSTRUCTIONS:

1. Blend orange and grapefruit segments, lime juice, honey, and sugar together in a blender.

2. Blend everything thoroughly up to it's smooth.

3. Over ice cubes, please.

NUTRITION (PER SERVING):

Cals: 70

Fat: 0g

Carbs: 18g

Fiber: 3g

Protein: 1g

359. VEGGIE HEAVEN

Time: 20 mins

Servings: 4

INGREDIENTS:

- 2 carrots, peel off and chop-up
- 2 tomatoes, chop-up
- 1 red bell pepper, chop-up
- 1 cucumber, peel off and chop-up
- 1 celery stalk, chop-up
- 1 cup of water
- Juice of 1 lemon
- Ice cubes

INSTRUCTIONS:

1. Blend carrots, tomatoes, red bell peppers, cucumbers, celery, water, and lemon juice together in a blender.

2. Blend everything thoroughly up to it's smooth.

3. Over ice cubes, please.

NUTRITION (PER SERVING):

Cals: 45

Fat: 0g

Carbs: 10g

Fiber: 3g

Protein: 1g

360. POWER BLEND

Time: 5 mins

Servings: 2

INGREDIENTS:

- 1 banana
- 1 cup of spinach leaves
- 1 tbsp almond butter
- 1 cup of almond milk
- Ice cubes

INSTRUCTIONS:

1. Banana, spinach leaves, almond butter, and almond milk Must all be mixd in a blender.

2. Blend everything thoroughly up to it's smooth.

3. Over ice cubes, please.

NUTRITION (PER SERVING):

Cals: 180

Fat: 8g

Carbs: 25g

Fiber: 4g

Protein: 5g

361.RAINBOW SPLASH

Time: 10 mins

Servings: 2

INGREDIENTS:

- 1 cup of chop-up pineapple
- 1 cup of chop-up watermelon
- 1 cup of chop-up mango
- 1 cup of coconut water
- Ice cubes

INSTRUCTIONS:

1. Mango, pineapple, watermelon, and coconut water Must all be mixd in a blender.

2. Blend everything thoroughly up to it's smooth.

3. Over ice cubes, please.

NUTRITION (PER SERVING):

Cals: 110

Fat: 1g

Carbs: 28g

Fiber: 4g

Protein: 1g

362.LEMONADE TWIST

Time: 5 mins

Servings: 2

INGREDIENTS:

- Juice of 4 lemons
- 2 cups of water
- 2 tbsp honey or sugar
- Ice cubes
- Lemon slices for garnish

INSTRUCTIONS:

1. Mix lemon juice, water, and honey or sugar in a pitcher.

2. Once the sweetener has dissolved, thoroughly stir.

3. Over ice cubes, please.

4. If desired, add lemon slices as a garnish.

NUTRITION (PER SERVING):

Cals: 45

Fat: 0g

Carbs: 14g

Fiber: 0g

Protein: 0g

363.ORANGE DELIGHT

Time: 5 mins

Servings: 2

INGREDIENTS:

- Juice of 4 oranges
- 1 tsp finely grated orange zest
- 1 cup of water
- 2 tbsp honey or sugar
- Ice cubes
- Orange slices for garnish

INSTRUCTIONS:

1. Orange juice, orange zest, water, and honey/sugar Must all be mixd in a pitcher.

2. Once the sweetener has dissolved, thoroughly stir.

3. Over ice cubes, please.

4. If desired, add orange slices as a garnish.

NUTRITION (PER SERVING):

Cals: 70

Fat: 0g

Carbs: 18g

Fiber: 0g

Protein: 0g

364.CARROT COOLER

Time: 10 mins

Servings: 2

INGREDIENTS:

- 2 carrots, peel off and chop-up
- 1 apple, cored and chop-up
- 1-inch piece of ginger, peel off
- 1 cup of water
- Juice of 1 lemon
- Ice cubes

INSTRUCTIONS:

1. Carrots, apple, ginger, water, and lemon juice Must all be put in a blender.

2. Blend everything thoroughly up to it's smooth.

3. Over ice cubes, please.

NUTRITION (PER SERVING):

Cals: 60

Fat: 0g

Carbs: 14g

Fiber: 3g

Protein: 1g

365.BEETROOT BEAUTY:

Time: 5 mins

Servings: 1

INGREDIENTS:

- 1 mini beetroot, peel off and chop-up
- 1 cup of refrigerate berries (e.g., strawberries, blueberries)
- 1 cup of almond milk
- 1 tbsp honey or maple syrup (non-compulsory)

INSTRUCTIONS:

1. Blend the items together in a blender.

2. Blend till creamy and smooth.

3. Pour into a glass, then serve right away.

NUTRITION INFO (APPROXIMATE):

Cals: 150

Carbs: 35g

Protein: 3g

Fat: 2g

Fiber: 6g

366. PINEAPPLE PASSION:

Time: 5 mins

Servings: 1

INGREDIENTS:

- 1 cup of pineapple chunks
- 1 banana
- 1/2 cup of coconut milk
- 1/2 cup of orange juice
- 1/2 tsp finely grated ginger

INSTRUCTIONS:

1. To a blender, add all the ingredients.

2. Blend till creamy and smooth.

3. Place in a glass and sip.

NUTRITION INFO (APPROXIMATE):

Cals: 220

Carbs: 52g

Protein: 3g

Fat: 4g

Fiber: 5g

367.MANGO MARVEL:

Time: 5 mins

Servings: 1

INGREDIENTS:

- 1 ripe mango, peel off and diced
- 1/2 cup of Greek yogurt
- 1/2 cup of orange juice
- 1/2 cup of almond milk
- 1 tbsp honey or agave syrup (non-compulsory)

INSTRUCTIONS:

1. Blend the items together in a blender.

2. Blend till creamy and smooth.

3. Pour cold liquid into a glass and serve.

NUTRITION INFO (APPROXIMATE):

Cals: 250

Carbs: 52g

Protein: 12g

Fat: 2g

Fiber: 5g

368. WATERMELON CRUSH:

Time: 5 mins

Servings: 1

INGREDIENTS:

- 2 cups of diced watermelon
- 1/2 cup of fresh lime juice
- 1/4 cup of fresh mint leaves
- 1 tbsp honey or agave syrup (non-compulsory)
- Ice cubes (non-compulsory)

INSTRUCTIONS:

1. Blend the items together in a blender.

2. Blend everything thoroughly up to it's smooth.

3. For a cold version, if preferred, add ice cubes and blend once more.

4. Put some mint leaves on top after pouring into a glass.

NUTRITION INFO (APPROXIMATE):

Cals: 100

Carbs: 26g

Protein: 1g

Fat: 0g

Fiber: 1g

369.GINGER FIRE:

Time: 5 mins

Servings: 1

INGREDIENTS:

- 1 inch piece of ginger, peel off and finely grated
- 1 cup of unsweetened almond milk
- 1 tbsp honey or maple syrup
- 1/2 tsp ground turmeric
- 1/2 tsp ground cinnamon

INSTRUCTIONS:

1. To a blender, add all the ingredients.

2. Blend up to foamy and well blended.

3. Pour into a glass, then serve right away.

NUTRITION INFO (APPROXIMATE):

Cals: 80

Carbs: 17g

Protein: 1g

Fat: 2g

Fiber: 2g

370.POMEGRANATE PUNCH:

Time: 5 mins

Servings: 1

INGREDIENTS:

- 1 cup of pomegranate seeds
- 1/2 cup of plain Greek yogurt
- 1/2 cup of cranberry juice
- 1/4 cup of almond milk
- 1 tbsp honey or agave syrup (non-compulsory)

INSTRUCTIONS:

1. Blend the items together in a blender.

2. Blend till creamy and smooth.

3. Place in a glass and sip.

NUTRITION INFO (APPROXIMATE):

Cals: 180

Carbs: 37g

Protein: 8g

Fat: 1g

Fiber: 4g

371.BLUEBERRY BLAST:

Time: 5 mins

Servings: 1

INGREDIENTS:

- 1 cup of blueberries
- 1/2 cup of vanilla yogurt
- 1/2 cup of almond milk
- 1 tbsp honey or maple syrup

INSTRUCTIONS:

1. To a blender, add all the ingredients.

2. Blend till creamy and smooth.

3. Pour cold liquid into a glass and serve.

NUTRITION INFO (APPROXIMATE):

Cals: 180

Carbs: 38g

Protein: 5g

Fat: 2g

Fiber: 6g

372.RASPBERRY RAPTURE:

Time: 5 mins

Servings: 1

INGREDIENTS:

- 1 cup of raspberries
- 1 banana
- 1/2 cup of coconut water
- 1/2 cup of almond milk
- 1 tbsp chia seeds

INSTRUCTIONS:

1. Blend the items together in a blender.

2. Blend everything thoroughly up to it's smooth.

3. Pour into a glass, then serve right away.

NUTRITION INFO (APPROXIMATE):

Cals: 200

Carbs: 43g

Protein: 5g

Fat: 4g

Fiber: 12g

373.CREAMY COCONUT:

Time: 5 mins

Servings: 1

INGREDIENTS:

- 1/2 cup of coconut milk
- 1/2 cup of pineapple chunks
- 1/2 banana
- 1/4 cup of shredded coconut
- 1 tbsp honey or agave syrup (non-compulsory)

INSTRUCTIONS:

1. To a blender, add all the ingredients.

2. Blend till creamy and smooth.

3. Place in a glass and sip.

NUTRITION INFO (APPROXIMATE):

Cals: 300

Carbs: 38g

Protein: 3g

Fat: 17g

Fiber: 4g

374. KIWI FUSION:

Time: 5 mins

Servings: 1

INGREDIENTS:

- 2 ripe kiwis, peel off and split
- 1/2 cup of spinach leaves
- 1/2 cup of cucumber, peel off and chop-up
- 1/2 cup of coconut water
- 1 tbsp lime juice
- 1 tbsp honey or agave syrup (non-compulsory)

INSTRUCTIONS:

1. Blend the items together in a blender.

2. Blend everything thoroughly up to it's smooth.

3. Pour cold liquid into a glass and serve.

NUTRITION INFO (APPROXIMATE):

Cals: 120

Carbs: 28g

Protein: 3g

Fat: 1g

Fiber: 6g

375. PEAR PERK:

Time: 15 mins

Servings: 2

INGREDIENTS:

- 2 ripe pears
- 1 cup of Greek yogurt
- 2 tbsp honey
- 1/4 cup of granola

INSTRUCTIONS:

1. Pears Must be cleaned and cored before being slice into thin wedges.
2. Greek yogurt and honey Must be combined well in a bowl.
3. Layer the yogurt mixture, granola, and pear slices in serving glasses or bowls.
4. Layers Must be repeated up to all of the ingredients are used.
5. Serve right away and delight in!

376. PEVERYY PLEASURE:

Time: 20 mins

Servings: 4

INGREDIENTS:

- 4 ripe peveryes
- 1 cup of vanilla ice cream
- 1/4 cup of chop-up almonds
- 2 tbsp honey

INSTRUCTIONS:

1. Take out the pits before halves the peveryes.
2. The peveryes Must be grilled for about five mins on every side, over medium heat, up to they are soft and have grill marks.
3. The peveryes Must be taken from the grill and given some time to cool.
4. Top every grilled pevery half with a spoonful of vanilla ice cream.

5. Sprinkle chop-up almonds and honey over the ice cream.
6. Serve right away and delight in!

377.STRAWBERRY DELIGHT:

Time: 10 mins

Servings: 2

INGREDIENTS:

- 2 cups of fresh strawberries, hulled and split
- 1 cup of whipped cream
- 2 tbsp powdered sugar
- 1 tsp vanilla extract

INSTRUCTIONS:

1. Whipping cream, powdered sugar, and vanilla extract Must all be mixd in a bowl. Mix thoroughly.
2. Layer the split strawberries and whipped cream mixture in serving cups of or bowls.
3. Layers Must be repeated up to all of the ingredients are used.
4. Serve right away and delight in!

378.MELON MINGLE:

Time: 15 mins

Servings: 4

INGREDIENTS:

- 2 cups of diced watermelon
- 2 cups of diced cantaloupe
- 2 cups of diced honeydew melon
- 1 tbsp fresh lime juice
- Fresh mint leaves for garnish

INSTRUCTIONS:

1. Mix the chop-up watermelon, cantaloupe, and honeydew melon in a big bowl.

2. Fresh lime juice Must be drizzled over the melon mixture, then gently combined in.
3. Serve in individual glasses or bowls and top with mint leaves that have just been picked.
4. Serve right away and delight in!

379.GOLDEN GODDESS:

Time: 30 mins

Servings: 6

INGREDIENTS:

- 2 Big mangoes, peel off and diced
- 1 cup of pineapple chunks
- 1 cup of diced papaya
- 1 cup of split banana
- 1/4 cup of fresh orange juice
- 1 tbsp finely grated coconut (non-compulsory)

INSTRUCTIONS:

1. Mix the chop-up mangoes, pineapple pieces, papaya, and split banana in a big bowl.
2. Fresh orange juice Must be drizzled over the fruit mixture before being gently combined in.
3. If desired, add finely grated coconut on top.
4. Before serving, let the food cool for at least an hr in the refrigerator.
5. Enjoy while serving chilled!

380.MINTY MELODY:

Time: 10 mins

Servings: 1

INGREDIENTS:

- 1 cup of fresh pineapple chunks
- 1/2 cup of fresh mint leaves
- 1/2 cup of coconut water
- 1 tbsp lime juice

- Ice cubes (non-compulsory)

INSTRUCTIONS:

1. Fresh pineapple chunks, mint leaves, coconut water, and lime juice Must all be put in a blender.
2. Blend everything thoroughly up to it's smooth.
3. If desired, add ice cubes and mix once more up to the mixture is cold.
4. Pour into a glass, then serve right away. Enjoy!

381.GREEN SYMPHONY:

Time: 15 mins

Servings: 2

INGREDIENTS:

- 2 cups of baby spinach
- 1 Big ripe banana
- 1/2 cup of chop-up cucumber
- 1/2 cup of chop-up green apple
- 1/2 cup of almond milk
- 1 tbsp honey (non-compulsory)

INSTRUCTIONS:

1. Blend the baby spinach, ripe banana, cucumber, green apple, almond milk, and honey (if using) in a blender.
2. Blend everything thoroughly up to it's smooth.
3. Pour into glasses and start serving right away. Enjoy!

382.BERRY BLISS:

Time: 10 mins

Servings: 2

INGREDIENTS:

- 1 cup of combined berries (strawberries, blueberries, raspberries)
- 1 cup of vanilla yogurt
- 2 tbsp honey
- 1/4 cup of granola

INSTRUCTIONS:

1. Layer the combined berries, vanilla yogurt, honey, and granola in serving glasses or bowls.
2. Layers Must be repeated up to all of the ingredients are used.
3. Serve right away and delight in!

383.CITRUS SPLASH:

Time: 10 mins

Servings: 2

INGREDIENTS:

- 2 oranges, peel off and segmented
- 1 grapefruit, peel off and segmented
- 1 lime, juiced
- 2 tbsp honey
- Fresh mint leaves for garnish

INSTRUCTIONS:

1. Orange and grapefruit segments, lime juice, and honey Must all be mixd in a bowl. Mix thoroughly.
2. Pour the citrus concoction into serving glasses or bowls.
3. Use fresh mint leaves as a garnish.
4. Serve right away and delight in!

384. VEGGIE WONDER:

Time: 25 mins

Servings: 4

INGREDIENTS:

- 2 zucchinis, spiralized
- 2 carrots, spiralized
- 1 red bell pepper, thinly split
- 1/2 cup of cherry tomatoes, halved
- 1/4 cup of chop-up fresh basil
- 2 tbsp olive oil
- 2 tbsp balsamic vinegar
- Salt and pepper as needed

INSTRUCTIONS:

1. Split red bell pepper, cherry tomatoes, spiralized zucchini, spiralized carrots, and fresh basil leaves Must all be mixd in a big bowl.
2. Mix the olive oil and balsamic vinegar in a mini bowl. Add salt and pepper as needed.
3. Over the vegetable combination, drizzle the dressing and give it a gentle swirl to coat.
4. Enjoy while serving chilled or at room temperature

385. POWER POTION:

Time: 5 mins

Servings: 1

INGREDIENTS:

- 1 cup of spinach
- 1/2 cup of kale
- 1/2 cucumber
- 1 green apple
- 1/2 lemon, juiced
- 1-inch piece of ginger
- 1 cup of coconut water

INSTRUCTIONS:

1. Thoroughly clean all the components.
2. Cucumber, apple, and ginger are peel off and chop-up.
3. Blend the spinach, kale, cucumber, apple, lemon juice, ginger, and coconut water together in a blender.
4. Blend everything thoroughly up to it's smooth.
5. Pour into a glass, then serve right away.

386.RAINBOW DELIGHT:

Time: 10 mins

Servings: 2

INGREDIENTS:

- 1 cup of refrigerate combined berries
- 1 ripe banana
- 1/2 cup of Greek yogurt
- 1/2 cup of almond milk
- 1 tbsp honey
- 1/2 tsp vanilla extract

INSTRUCTIONS:

1. Blend the items together in a blender.
2. Blend till creamy and smooth.
3. Pour cold liquid into glasses and serve.

387.LEMON LIME DELIGHT:

Time: 5 mins

Servings: 1

INGREDIENTS:

- 1 lemon, juiced
- 1 lime, juiced
- 1 tbsp honey

- 1 cup of sparkling water
- Ice cubes

INSTRUCTIONS:

1. Honey, lime juice, and lemon juice Must all be mixd in a glass.
2. Stir the honey up to it dissolves.
3. To the glass, add ice cubes.
4. Along with the ice cubes, pour sparkling water.
5. Serve after a gentle stir.

388.ORANGE ZEST:

Time: 5 mins

Servings: 1

INGREDIENTS:

- 1 orange, peel off and segmented
- 1/2 cup of plain yogurt
- 1 tbsp honey
- 1/4 tsp vanilla extract
- Ice cubes

INSTRUCTIONS:

1. Orange segments, yogurt, honey, and vanilla essence Must all be blended together.
2. Up to smooth, blend.
3. In a glass, put few ice cubes.
4. Over the ice cubes, pour the orange mixture.
5. Stir gently, then devour.

389.CARROT KICK:

Time: 7 mins

Servings: 1

INGREDIENTS:

- 1 Big carrot, peel off and chop-up
- 1 orange, peel off and segmented
- 1/2 cup of pineapple chunks
- 1/2 cup of coconut water
- Ice cubes

INSTRUCTIONS:

1. Blend the carrot, pineapple chunks, orange segments, and coconut water together in a blender.
2. Up to smooth, blend.
3. In a glass, put few ice cubes.
4. Over the ice cubes, pour the carrot mixture.
5. Serve after a gentle stir.

390.BEETROOT BLAST:

Time: 8 mins

Servings: 1

INGREDIENTS:

- 1 mini beetroot, peel off and chop-up
- 1/2 cup of strawberries
- 1/2 cup of plain Greek yogurt
- 1 tbsp honey
- 1/2 cup of almond milk
- Ice cubes

INSTRUCTIONS:

1. Beetroot, strawberries, yogurt, honey, and almond milk Must all be mixd in a blender.

2. Blend till creamy and smooth.
3. In a glass, put few ice cubes.
4. Over the ice cubes, pour the beetroot mixture.
5. Stir gently, then devour.

391.PINEAPPLE DELIGHT:

Time: 5 mins

Servings: 1

INGREDIENTS:

- 1 cup of chop-up pineapple
- 1/2 cup of coconut milk
- 1/2 cup of pineapple juice
- 1/4 cup of ice cubes

INSTRUCTIONS:

1. The diced pineapple, coconut milk, pineapple juice, and ice cubes Must all be blended together.
2. Blend up to foamy and well-mixd.
3. Pour cold liquid into a glass and serve.

392.MANGO MADNESS:

Time: 5 mins

Servings: 1

INGREDIENTS:

- 1 ripe mango, peel off and chop-up
- 1/2 cup of mango juice
- 1/2 cup of Greek yogurt
- 1 tbsp honey
- Ice cubes

INSTRUCTIONS:

1. Mango chunks, mango juice, Greek yogurt, honey, and ice cubes Must all be mixd in a blender.
2. Blend till creamy and smooth.
3. Pour cold liquid into a glass and serve.

393.WATERMELON WONDER:

Time: 5 mins

Servings: 1

INGREDIENTS:

- 1 cup of cubed watermelon
- 1/2 cup of coconut water
- 1/2 lime, juiced
- Fresh mint leaves (non-compulsory)
- Ice cubes

INSTRUCTIONS:

1. The watermelon, coconut water, lime juice, and a few mint leaves (non-compulsory) Must all be blended together.
2. Up to smooth, blend.
3. In a glass, put few ice cubes.
4. Over the ice cubes, pour the watermelon mixture.
5. Serve after a gentle stir.

394.GINGER CRUSH:

Time: 5 mins

Servings: 1

INGREDIENTS:

- 1-inch piece of ginger, peel off
- 1/2 cup of orange juice
- 1/2 cup of apple juice

- 1 tbsp honey
- Ice cubes

INSTRUCTIONS:

1. Use a fine grater or zester to shred the ginger before blending it.
2. Ginger, apple juice, orange juice, honey, and ice cubes Must all be added to the blender.
3. Blend everything thoroughly.
4. Pour cold liquid into a glass and serve.

395.POMEGRANATE PASSION:

Time: 10 mins

Servings: 2

INGREDIENTS:

- 2 cups of pomegranate seeds
- 1 cup of pineapple juice
- 1 tbsp honey
- Ice cubes

INSTRUCTIONS:

1. Pomegranate seeds, pineapple juice, honey, and a few ice cubes Must all be blended together.
2. Blend everything thoroughly up to it's smooth.
3. Pour cold liquid into glasses and serve.

396.BLUEBERRY BREEZE:

Time: 15 mins

Servings: 4

INGREDIENTS:

- 2 cups of blueberries
- 1 cup of almond milk
- 1 banana

- 1 tbsp chia seeds
- Honey (non-compulsory, for sweetness)
- Ice cubes

INSTRUCTIONS:

1. Blueberries, almond milk, banana, chia seeds, honey (if wanted), and a few ice cubes Must all be blended together.
2. Blend till creamy and smooth.
3. Fill glasses with liquid and sip.

397. RASPBERRY REFRESH:

Time: 10 mins

Servings: 2

INGREDIENTS:

- 2 cups of raspberries
- 1 cup of coconut water
- 1 tbsp lime juice
- Mint leaves (for garnish)
- Ice cubes

INSTRUCTIONS:

1. Raspberries, coconut water, lime juice, and a few ice cubes Must all be blended together.
2. Blend everything thoroughly.
3. Serve chilled after pouring into glasses and adding mint leaves as a garnish.

398. CREAMY DREAM:

Time: 5 mins

Servings: 1

INGREDIENTS:

- 1 ripe avocado
- 1 cup of unsweetened almond milk
- 1 tbsp honey or maple syrup
- 1 tsp vanilla extract
- Ice cubes

INSTRUCTIONS:

1. Avocado, almond milk, honey (or maple syrup), vanilla extract, and a few ice cubes Must all be mixd in a blender.
2. Blend up to smooth and creamy.
3. Place in a glass and sip.

399. KIWI SPARKLE:

Time: 10 mins

Servings: 2

INGREDIENTS:

- 4 kiwis, peel off and chop-up
- 1 cup of sparkling water
- 1 tbsp lime juice
- 1 tbsp agave syrup or honey
- Ice cubes

INSTRUCTIONS:

1. Kiwis, sparkling water, lime juice, agave syrup (or honey), and a few ice cubes Must all be mixd in a blender.
2. Blend everything thoroughly.
3. Pour cold liquid into glasses and serve.

400.PEAR PLEASER:

Time: 10 mins

Servings: 2

INGREDIENTS:

- 2 ripe pears, peel off and diced
- 1 cup of unsweetened almond milk
- 1 tbsp honey or maple syrup
- 1/2 tsp ground cinnamon
- Ice cubes

INSTRUCTIONS:

1. Pears, almond milk, honey (or maple syrup), ground cinnamon, and a few ice cubes Must all be mixd in a blender.
2. Blend till creamy and smooth.
3. Fill glasses with liquid and sip.

401.PEVERYY PUNCH:

Time: 10 mins

Servings: 2

INGREDIENTS:

- 2 ripe peveryes, peel off and split
- 1 cup of orange juice
- 1/2 cup of Greek yogurt
- 1 tbsp honey
- Ice cubes

INSTRUCTIONS:

1. Blend peveryes, orange juice, Greek yogurt, honey, and a few ice cubes together in a blender.
2. Blend up to smooth and well incorporated.
3. Pour cold liquid into glasses and serve.

402.STRAWBERRY SURPRISE:

Time: 15 mins

Servings: 4

INGREDIENTS:

- 2 cups of strawberries
- 1 cup of coconut milk
- 1 banana
- 1 tbsp flaxseeds
- 1 tbsp honey or agave syrup
- Ice cubes

INSTRUCTIONS:

1. Strawberries, coconut milk, banana, flaxseeds, honey (or agave syrup), and a few ice cubes Must all be mixd in a blender.
2. Blend till creamy and smooth.
3. Fill glasses with liquid and sip.

403.MELON MAGIC:

Time: 10 mins

Servings: 2

INGREDIENTS:

- 2 cups of diced watermelon
- 1 cup of cucumber slices
- 1 tbsp lime juice
- 1 tbsp fresh mint leaves
- Ice cubes

INSTRUCTIONS:

1. Cucumber slices, watermelon, lime juice, mint leaves, and a few ice cubes Must all be mixd in a blender.
2. Blend everything thoroughly and smoothly.

3. Serve chilled after pouring into glasses and adding mint leaves as a garnish.

404. GOLDEN GLOW:

Time: 5 mins

Servings: 1

INGREDIENTS:

- 1 cup of fresh orange juice
- 1/2 cup of pineapple chunks
- 1/2 tsp turmeric powder
- 1/2 tsp finely grated ginger
- Ice cubes

INSTRUCTIONS:

1. Orange juice, pineapple chunks, ginger, turmeric, and a few ice cubes Must all be blended together.
2. Blend everything thoroughly.
3. Place in a glass and sip.

405. MINTY COOL:

Time: 5 mins

Servings: 1

INGREDIENTS:

- 1 cup of fresh mint leaves
- 1 lime, juiced
- 2 tbsp honey
- 1 cup of cold water
- Ice cubes

INSTRUCTIONS:

1. Fresh mint leaves, lime juice, honey, and water Must all be put in a blender.

2. Up to smooth, blend.

3. Pour into a glass with ice cubes, then top with a mint sprig for decoration.

4. Offer cold.

NUTRITION:

Cals: 70

Carbs: 19g

Fat: 0g

Protein: 1g

Fiber: 2g

406.GREEN ENERGY:

Time: 10 mins

Servings: 1

INGREDIENTS:

- 1 cup of spinach
- 1 banana
- 1/2 cup of pineapple chunks
- 1/2 cup of coconut water
- 1 tbsp chia seeds (non-compulsory)
- Ice cubes

INSTRUCTIONS:

1. Blend spinach, banana, pineapple pieces, coconut water, and chia seeds in a food processor.

2. Up to smooth, blend.

3. When the appropriate consistency is attained, add ice cubes and mix once more.

4. To serve, pour into a glass.

NUTRITION:

Cals: 220

Carbs: 51g

Fat: 2g

Protein: 5g

Fiber: 10g

407.BERRY BURST:

Time: 5 mins

Servings: 2

INGREDIENTS:

- 1 cup of combined berries (strawberries, blueberries, raspberries)
- 1/2 cup of Greek yogurt
- 1 cup of almond milk (or any other milk of your choice)
- 1 tbsp honey (non-compulsory)
- Ice cubes

INSTRUCTIONS:

1. Greek yogurt, almond milk, honey, and combined berries Must all be mixd in a blender.

2. Up to smooth, blend.

3. When the appropriate consistency is attained, add ice cubes and mix once more.

4. Pour cold liquid into glasses and serve.

NUTRITION (PER SERVING):

Cals: 120

Carbs: 19g

Fat: 3g

Protein: 6g

Fiber: 4g

408.CITRUS BLAST:

Time: 5 mins

Servings: 1

INGREDIENTS:

- 1 orange, peel off and segmented
- 1 grapefruit, peel off and segmented
- 1 lemon, juiced
- 1 tsp honey (non-compulsory)
- Ice cubes

INSTRUCTIONS:

1. Orange, grapefruit, lemon, and honey segments are mixd in a blender.

2. Up to smooth, blend.

3. When the appropriate consistency is attained, add ice cubes and mix once more.

4. Pour cold liquid into a glass and serve.

NUTRITION:

Cals: 90

Carbs: 22g

Fat: 0g

Protein: 2g

Fiber: 4g

409.VEGGIE INFUSION:

Time: 10 mins

Servings: 2

INGREDIENTS:

- 1 cucumber, peel off and split
- 2 stalks celery, chop-up
- 1 green apple, cored and chop-up
- 1/2 lemon, juiced
- 1 cup of water
- Ice cubes

INSTRUCTIONS:

1. Cucumber slices, celery, green apple, lemon juice, and water Must all be put in a blender.

2. Up to smooth, blend.

3. When the appropriate consistency is attained, add ice cubes and mix once more.

4. Pour cold liquid into glasses and serve.

NUTRITION (PER SERVING):

Cals: 60

Carbs: 15g

Fat: 0g

Protein: 1g

Fiber: 3g

410.POWER PUNCH:

Time: 5 mins

Servings: 1

INGREDIENTS:

- 1 cup of combined berries (strawberries, blueberries, raspberries)
- 1 banana
- 1/2 cup of orange juice
- 1/2 cup of almond milk (or any other milk of your choice)
- 1 tbsp protein powder (non-compulsory)
- Ice cubes

INSTRUCTIONS:

1. Blend the combined berries, banana, orange juice, almond milk, and protein powder together in a blender.

2. Up to smooth, blend.

3. When the appropriate consistency is attained, add ice cubes and mix once more.

4. Pour cold liquid into a glass and serve.

NUTRITION:

Cals: 280

Carbs: 58g

Fat: 3g

Protein: 10g

Fiber: 10g

411.RAINBOW BLEND:

Time: 10 mins

Servings: 2

INGREDIENTS:

- 1 cup of chop-up watermelon
- 1 cup of chop-up pineapple
- 1 cup of chop-up mango
- 1 cup of spinach
- 1 cup of coconut water
- Ice cubes

INSTRUCTIONS:

1. Watermelon, pineapple, mango, spinach, and coconut water Must all be mixd in a blender.

2. Up to smooth, blend.

3. When the appropriate consistency is attained, add ice cubes and mix once more.

4. Pour cold liquid into glasses and serve.

NUTRITION (PER SERVING):

Cals: 140

Carbs: 34g

Fat: 1g

Protein: 3g

Fiber: 6g

412.LEMONADE FIZZ:

Time: 5 mins

Servings: 2

INGREDIENTS:

- 2 lemons, juiced
- 2 cups of sparkling water
- 2 tbsp honey (or more as needed)
- Fresh mint leaves for garnish
- Ice cubes

INSTRUCTIONS:

1. Lemon juice, sparkling water, and honey Must all be put in a pitcher.

2. Up to honey is dissolved, stir thoroughly.

3. Pour the lemonade over the ice in serving glasses after adding ice cubes.

4. Serve with fresh mint leaves as a garnish.

NUTRITION (PER SERVING):

Cals: 40

Carbs: 11g

Fat: 0g

Protein: 0g

Fiber: 1g

413.ORANGE CRUSH:

Time: 5 mins

Servings: 1

INGREDIENTS:

- 2 oranges, peel off and segmented
- 1/2 cup of coconut water
- 1 tbsp agave syrup (or any other sweetener of your choice)
- Ice cubes

INSTRUCTIONS:

1. Orange segments, coconut water, and agave syrup Must all be blended together.

2. Up to smooth, blend.

3. When the appropriate consistency is attained, add ice cubes and mix once more.

4. Pour cold liquid into a glass and serve.

NUTRITION:

Cals: 120

Carbs: 29g

Fat: 0g

Protein: 2g

Fiber: 5g

414.CARROT CRAZE:

Time: 10 mins

Servings: 2

INGREDIENTS:

- 2 Big carrots, peel off and chop-up
- 1 orange, peel off and segmented
- 1 inch fresh ginger, peel off and finely grated
- 1 cup of water
- 1 tbsp honey (non-compulsory)
- Ice cubes

INSTRUCTIONS:

1. Chop-up carrots, orange segments, finely grated ginger, water, and honey are mixd in a blender.

2. Up to smooth, blend.

3. When the appropriate consistency is attained, add ice cubes and mix once more.

4. Pour cold liquid into glasses and serve.

NUTRITION (PER SERVING):

Cals: 70

Carbs: 17g

Fat: 0g

Protein: 1g

Fiber: 3g

415.BEETROOT BEAUTY

Time: 20 mins

Servings: 2

INGREDIENTS:

- 2 medium-sized beetroots, peel off and chop-up
- 1 apple, cored and chop-up
- 1 carrot, peel off and chop-up
- 1 celery stalk, chop-up
- 1-inch piece of ginger, finely grated
- 1 cup of water
- Ice cubes (non-compulsory)

INSTRUCTIONS:

1. Beetroots, apple, carrot, celery, ginger, and water Must all be put in a blender.

2. Blend up to creamy and smooth on high.

3. To make it cooled, if required, add ice cubes and blend once more.

4. Pour into glasses, then offer.

NUTRITION INFO (PER SERVING):

Cals: 120

Carbs: 28g

Protein: 2g

Fat: 0.5g

Fiber: 6g

416. PINEAPPLE PARADISE

Time: 10 mins

Servings: 2

INGREDIENTS:

- 2 cups of fresh pineapple chunks
- 1 ripe banana
- 1 cup of coconut water
- 1 tbsp of honey (non-compulsory)
- Ice cubes (non-compulsory)

INSTRUCTIONS:

1. Blend the pineapple chunks, banana, coconut water, and honey (if using) together in a blender.

2. Blend up to creamy and smooth on high.

3. To make it cooled, if required, add ice cubes and blend once more.

4. Pour into glasses, then offer.

NUTRITION INFO (PER SERVING):

Cals: 150

Carbs: 38g

Protein: 2g

Fat: 0.5g

Fiber: 4g

417.MANGO MANIA

Time: 15 mins

Servings: 2

INGREDIENTS:

- 2 ripe mangoes, peel off and diced
- 1 cup of orange juice
- 1 cup of plain yogurt (or coconut milk for a vegan option)
- 1 tbsp of honey (non-compulsory)
- Ice cubes (non-compulsory)

INSTRUCTIONS:

1. Mango dice, orange juice, yogurt (or coconut milk), and honey (if using) Must all be mixd in a blender.

2. Blend up to creamy and smooth on high.

3. To make it cooled, if required, add ice cubes and blend once more.

4. Pour into glasses, then offer.

NUTRITION INFO (PER SERVING):

Cals: 220

Carbs: 48g

Protein: 4g

Fat: 1g

Fiber: 3g

418. WATERMELON SPLASH

Time: 10 mins

Servings: 2

INGREDIENTS:

- 3 cups of fresh watermelon, seeded and cubed
- 1 cup of coconut water
- Juice of 1 lime
- Mint leaves for garnish (non-compulsory)
- Ice cubes (non-compulsory)

INSTRUCTIONS:

1. Cubed watermelon, coconut water, and lime juice Must all be mixd in a blender.

2. Blend up to creamy and smooth on high.

3. To make it cooled, if required, add ice cubes and blend once more.

4. Pour into glasses, add mint leaves as a garnish (if desired), and serve.

NUTRITION INFO (PER SERVING):

Cals: 80

Carbs: 20g

Protein: 2g

Fat: 0.5g

Fiber: 1g

419.GINGER ZING

Time: 10 mins

Servings: 1

INGREDIENTS:

- 1 cup of fresh orange juice
- 1 tbsp of finely grated ginger
- 1 tbsp of honey (non-compulsory)
- Ice cubes (non-compulsory)

INSTRUCTIONS:

1. Orange juice, finely grated ginger, and honey (if using) Must all be mixd in a blender.

2. Blend everything thoroughly on high.

3. To make it cooled, if required, add ice cubes and blend once more.

4. To serve, pour into a glass.

NUTRITION INFO (PER SERVING):

Cals: 80

Carbs: 20g

Protein: 1g

Fat: 0g

Fiber: 1g

420. POMEGRANATE POWER

Time: 15 mins

Servings: 2

INGREDIENTS:

- 2 cups of pomegranate arils
- 1 cup of almond milk (or any other plant-based milk)
- 1 tbsp of honey (non-compulsory)
- Ice cubes (non-compulsory)

INSTRUCTIONS:

1. The pomegranate arils, almond milk, and honey (if used) Must all be mixd in a blender.

2. Blend up to creamy and smooth on high.

3. To make it cooled, if required, add ice cubes and blend once more.

4. Pour into glasses, then offer.

NUTRITION INFO (PER SERVING):

Cals: 150

Carbs: 34g

Protein: 2g

Fat: 3g

Fiber: 6g

421.BLUEBERRY BLISS

Time: 10 mins

Servings: 2

INGREDIENTS:

- 2 cups of fresh blueberries
- 1 cup of unsweetened almond milk (or any other plant-based milk)
- 1 tbsp of maple syrup (non-compulsory)
- Ice cubes (non-compulsory)

INSTRUCTIONS:

1. The blueberries, almond milk, and maple syrup (if used) Must all be mixd in a blender.

2. Blend up to creamy and smooth on high.

3. To make it cooled, if required, add ice cubes and blend once more.

4. Pour into glasses, then offer.

NUTRITION INFO (PER SERVING):

Cals: 120

Carbs: 26g

Protein: 2g

Fat: 2g

Fiber: 5g

422.RASPBERRY REVIVE

Time: 10 mins

Servings: 2

INGREDIENTS:

- 2 cups of fresh raspberries
- 1 cup of coconut water
- Juice of 1 lemon
- 1 tbsp of agave syrup (non-compulsory)
- Ice cubes (non-compulsory)

INSTRUCTIONS:

1. Raspberries, coconut water, lemon juice, and agave syrup (if used) Must all be mixd in a blender.

2. Blend up to creamy and smooth on high.

3. To make it cooled, if required, add ice cubes and blend once more.

4. Pour into glasses, then offer.

NUTRITION INFO (PER SERVING):

Cals: 90

Carbs: 21g

Protein: 2g

Fat: 1g

Fiber: 8g

423.CREAMY SUNSHINE

Time: 10 mins

Servings: 2

INGREDIENTS:

- 2 ripe bananas
- 1 cup of orange juice
- 1/2 cup of Greek yogurt (or any other yogurt of your choice)
- 1 tbsp of honey (non-compulsory)
- Ice cubes (non-compulsory)

INSTRUCTIONS:

1. Bananas, orange juice, yogurt, and honey (if using) Must all be mixd in a blender.

2. Blend up to creamy and smooth on high.

3. To make it cooled, if required, add ice cubes and blend once more.

4. Pour into glasses, then offer.

NUTRITION INFO (PER SERVING):

Cals: 180

Carbs: 42g

Protein: 5g

Fat: 1g

Fiber: 3g

424.KIWI CRUSH

Time: 10 mins

Servings: 2

INGREDIENTS:

- 4 ripe kiwis, peel off and split
- 1 cup of pineapple juice
- 1/2 cup of coconut milk
- 1 tbsp of lime juice
- Ice cubes (non-compulsory)

INSTRUCTIONS:

1. The kiwis, lime juice, coconut milk, and pineapple juice Must all be mixd in a blender.

2. Blend up to creamy and smooth on high.

3. To make it cooled, if required, add ice cubes and blend once more.

4. Pour into glasses, then offer.

NUTRITION INFO (PER SERVING):

Cals: 160

Carbs: 37g

Protein: 3g

Fat: 2g

Fiber: 6g

425.PEAR PLEASURE:

Time: 15 mins

Servings: 2

INGREDIENTS:

- 2 ripe pears, peel off and split
- 1 cup of Greek yogurt
- 2 tbsp honey
- 1/4 cup of chop-up walnuts

INSTRUCTIONS:

1. Greek yogurt and honey Must be thoroughly blended in a bowl.
2. In bowls or serving glasses, arrange the pear slices in layers.
3. Overlay the pears with the yogurt mixture.
4. On top, scatter the chop-up walnuts.
5. Dispense and savor!

426.PEVERYY PARADISE:

Time: 10 mins

Servings: 1

INGREDIENTS:

- 1 ripe pevery, pitted and split
- 1/2 cup of coconut milk
- 1 tbsp chia seeds
- 1 tbsp shredded coconut

INSTRUCTIONS:

1. Place the pevery slices in layers in a glass or jar.
2. Over the peveryes, pour the coconut milk.
3. Top with the chia seeds and coconut shavings.
4. To blend, thoroughly stir.
5. Let the chia seeds to absorb the liquid by letting it sit for 5 mins.

6. Offer cold.

427.STRAWBERRY SWIRL:

Time: 20 mins

Servings: 4

INGREDIENTS:

- 2 cups of refrigerate strawberries
- 1 banana
- 1 cup of almond milk
- 1 tbsp honey (non-compulsory)

INSTRUCTIONS:

1. Blend the refrigerate strawberries, banana, almond milk, and honey (if using) in a blender.
2. Blend till creamy and smooth.
3. Pour the mixture into bowls or serving glasses.
4. Make a swirling design with a spoon.
5. Offer cold.

428.MELON MADNESS:

Time: 10 mins

Servings: 2

INGREDIENTS:

- 2 cups of diced combined melons (watermelon, cantaloupe, honeydew)
- 1/2 cup of fresh mint leaves, chop-up
- 1 lime, juiced
- 1 tbsp honey

INSTRUCTIONS:

1. The diced melons and slice mint leaves Must be mixd in a bowl.
2. Pour honey and lime juice over the melon mixture.

3. To coat, gently toss.
4. Serve right away.

429.GOLDEN GODDESS:

Time: 15 mins

Servings: 2

INGREDIENTS:

- 2 ripe mangoes, peel off and diced
- 1 cup of pineapple chunks
- 1/2 cup of orange juice
- 1 tbsp turmeric powder

INSTRUCTIONS:

1. Mango dice, pineapple chunks, orange juice, and turmeric powder Must all be mixd in a blender.
2. Blend till creamy and smooth.
3. Pour into glasses for serving.
4. Offer cold.

430.MINTY FRESHNESS:

Time: 5 mins

Servings: 1

INGREDIENTS:

- 1 cup of spinach leaves
- 1 cup of fresh mint leaves
- 1/2 cucumber, peel off and split
- 1 green apple, cored and chop-up
- 1 tbsp lemon juice
- 1 cup of water

1. The spinach leaves, mint leaves, cucumber slices, green apple, lemon juice, and water Must all be put in a blender.
2. Blend everything thoroughly up to it's smooth.
3. Put some in a glass.
4. Offer cold.

431.GREEN POWER:

Time: 10 mins

Servings: 2

INGREDIENTS:

- 2 cups of kale leaves, chop-up
- 1 cup of pineapple chunks
- 1/2 cup of coconut water
- 1 tbsp flax seeds

INSTRUCTIONS:

1. The kale leaves, pineapple chunks, coconut water, and flax seeds Must all be mixd in a blender.
2. Up to smooth, blend.
3. Pour into glasses for serving.
4. Offer cold.

432.BERRY BONANZA:

Time: 15 mins

Servings: 2

INGREDIENTS:

- 1 cup of combined berries (strawberries, blueberries, raspberries)
- 1 banana
- 1 cup of almond milk
- 1 tbsp honey (non-compulsory)

INSTRUCTIONS:

1. The combined berries, banana, almond milk, and honey (if used) Must all be blended together.
2. Blend till creamy and smooth.
3. Pour into glasses for serving.
4. Offer cold.

433.CITRUS SYMPHONY:

Time: 10 mins

Servings: 2

INGREDIENTS:

- 2 oranges, peel off and segmented
- 1 grapefruit, peel off and segmented
- 1 lemon, juiced
- 1 tbsp honey

INSTRUCTIONS:

1. Mix the orange and grapefruit segments in a bowl.
2. Honey and lemon juice Must be drizzled over the citrus fruits.
3. Gently blend by tossing.
4. Offer cold.

434.VEGGIE VITALITY:

Time: 15 mins

Servings: 2

INGREDIENTS:

- 2 carrots, peel off and chop-up
- 2 stalks celery, chop-up
- 1 beet, peel off and chop-up
- 1/2 lemon, juiced
- 1 cup of water

INSTRUCTIONS:

1. Chop-up carrots, celery, beet, lemon juice, and water Must all be added to a blender.
2. Blend everything thoroughly up to it's smooth.
3. Pour into glasses for serving.
4. Offer cold.

435.POWER FUEL

Time: 10 mins

Servings: 2

INGREDIENTS:

- 2 ripe bananas
- 1 cup of spinach
- 1 cup of almond milk
- 1 tbsp chia seeds
- 1 tbsp honey

INSTRUCTIONS:

1. Bananas Must be peel off and added to a blender.

2. To the blender, add the spinach, almond milk, chia seeds, and honey.

3. Blend till creamy and smooth.

4. Pour into glasses and start serving right away.

NUTRITION INFO PER SERVING:

Cals: 180

Protein: 4g

Fat: 4g

Carbs: 35g

Fiber: 7g

536.RAINBOW REFRESHER

Time: 15 mins

Servings: 4

INGREDIENTS:

- 1 cup of diced watermelon
- 1 cup of diced pineapple
- 1 cup of diced cantaloupe
- 1 cup of diced honeydew melon
- 1 cup of blueberries
- 1 tbsp lime juice
- Mint leaves for garnish (non-compulsory)

INSTRUCTIONS:

1. The watermelon, pineapple, cantaloupe, honeydew melon, and blueberries Must all be mixd in a big bowl.

2. Add lime juice to the fruit, then toss it together gently.

3. If desired, add mint leaves as a garnish.

4. Offer cold.

NUTRITION INFO PER SERVING:

Cals: 80

Protein: 1g

Fat: 0g

Carbs: 20g

Fiber: 3g

437. LEMON LIME FIZZ

Time: 5 mins

Servings: 1

INGREDIENTS:

- Juice of 1 lemon
- Juice of 1 lime
- 1 tsp honey
- Sparkling water

INSTRUCTIONS:

1. Honey, lime juice, and lemon juice Must all be mixd in a glass.

2. Stir the honey up to it dissolves.

3. Spritz some sparkling water into the glass.

4. Gently stir, then serve cold.

NUTRITION INFO PER SERVING:

Cals: 30

Protein: 0g

Fat: 0g

Carbs: 8g

Fiber: 0g

438.ORANGE OASIS

Time: 10 mins

Servings: 2

INGREDIENTS:

- 2 Big oranges
- 1 cup of coconut water
- 1 tbsp agave nectar
- Ice cubes

INSTRUCTIONS:

1. Orange juice Must be squeezed out and added to a blender.

2. Blender with coconut water and agave nectar added.

3. Blend everything thoroughly.

4. Place ice cubes in glasses and then pour the orange concoction over them.

5. Gently stir, then serve cold.

NUTRITION INFO PER SERVING:

Cals: 80

Protein: 1g

Fat: 0g

Carbs: 20g

Fiber: 2g

439.CARROT CRUNCH

Time: 20 mins

Servings: 4

INGREDIENTS:

- 4 Big carrots, peel off and finely grated
- 1/4 cup of raisins
- 1/4 cup of chop-up walnuts
- 2 tbsp lemon juice
- 1 tbsp olive oil
- Salt and pepper as needed

INSTRUCTIONS:

1. The finely grated carrots, raisins, and chop-up walnuts Must all be mixd in a big basin.

2. Mix the lemon juice, olive oil, salt, and pepper in a mini bowl.

3. The dressing Must be poured over the carrot mixture, then thoroughly combined in.

4. To let the flavors to mingle, let the salad sit for 10 mins.

5. Offer cold.

NUTRITION INFO PER SERVING:

Cals: 120

Protein: 2g

Fat: 8g

Carbs: 11g

Fiber: 3g

440.BEETROOT BLAST

Time: 15 mins

Servings: 2

INGREDIENTS:

- 2 medium beets, peel off and finely grated
- 1 medium apple, finely grated
- 1/2 cup of plain Greek yogurt
- 1 tbsp honey
- 1/2 tsp finely grated ginger

INSTRUCTIONS:

1. The apple and finely grated beets Must be mixd in a bowl.

2. Mix the Greek yogurt, honey, and finely grated ginger in a another bowl.

3. Over the beet and apple mixture, pour the yogurt mixture.

4. To blend, thoroughly stir.

5. Offer cold.

NUTRITION INFO PER SERVING:

Cals: 120

Protein: 5g

Fat: 0g

Carbs: 26g

Fiber: 5g

441.PINEAPPLE PARTY

Time: 10 mins

Servings: 2

INGREDIENTS:

- 2 cups of fresh pineapple chunks
- 1 cup of coconut milk
- 1/2 cup of orange juice
- 1 tbsp honey
- Ice cubes

INSTRUCTIONS:

1. Blend together the pineapple pieces, orange juice, honey, and coconut milk.

2. Blend till creamy and smooth.

3. Place ice cubes in glasses and then pour the pineapple mixture over them.

4. Gently stir, then serve cold.

NUTRITION INFO PER SERVING:

Cals: 180

Protein: 1g

Fat: 8g

Carbs: 30g

Fiber: 3g

442.MANGO MAGIC

Time: 10 mins

Servings: 2

INGREDIENTS:

- 2 ripe mangoes, peel off and pitted
- 1 cup of almond milk
- 1 tbsp lime juice
- 1 tbsp honey
- Ice cubes

INSTRUCTIONS:

1. Blend the mango flesh after Cutting it into bits.

2. Blender ingredients: Almond milk, honey, and lime juice.

3. Blend till creamy and smooth.

4. Place ice cubes in glasses and then pour the mango mixture over them.

5. Gently stir, then serve cold.

NUTRITION INFO PER SERVING:

Cals: 180

Protein: 3g

Fat: 3g

Carbs: 40g

Fiber: 4g

443. WATERMELON WAVE

Time: 5 mins

Servings: 2

INGREDIENTS:

- 2 cups of diced watermelon
- 1 tbsp lime juice
- Fresh mint leaves for garnish (non-compulsory)

INSTRUCTIONS:

1. Lime juice and chop-up watermelon Must be blended together.

2. Up to smooth, blend.

3. Pour into glasses and, if preferred, garnish with fresh mint leaves.

4. Offer cold.

NUTRITION INFO PER SERVING:

Cals: 80

Protein: 1g

Fat: 0g

Carbs: 20g

Fiber: 1g

444.GINGER SNAP

Time: 5 mins

Servings: 1

INGREDIENTS:

- 1 cup of sparkling water
- 1 tbsp ginger syrup
- 1 tbsp lemon juice
- Ice cubes

INSTRUCTIONS:

1. Mix the lemon juice, ginger syrup, and sparkling water in a glass.

2. Stir thoroughly to mix.

3. Ice cubes Must be put in the glass.

4. Gently stir, then serve cold.

NUTRITION INFO PER SERVING:

Cals: 10

Protein: 0g

Fat: 0g

Carbs: 3g

Fiber: 0g

445. POMEGRANATE PLEASURE:

Time: 10 mins

Servings: 2

INGREDIENTS:

- 1 cup of pomegranate seeds
- 1 cup of plain yogurt
- 1 tbsp honey

INSTRUCTIONS:

1. Pomegranate seeds, yogurt, and honey Must all be mixd in a blender.

2. Blend everything thoroughly up to it's smooth.

3. Pour into serving glasses and, if preferred, top with more pomegranate seeds.

NUTRITION PER SERVING:

Cals: 150

Protein: 7g

Fat: 2g

Carbs: 30g

446. BLUEBERRY BLAST:

Time: 15 mins

Servings: 2

INGREDIENTS:

- 1 cup of blueberries
- 1 cup of almond milk
- 1 banana
- 1 tbsp chia seeds

- 1 tsp honey (non-compulsory)

INSTRUCTIONS:

1. Banana, chia seeds, honey, almond milk, and blueberries are all mixd in a blender.

2. Blend till creamy and smooth.

3. Pour cold liquid into glasses and serve.

NUTRITION PER SERVING:

Cals: 180

Protein: 4g

Fat: 4g

Carbs: 35g

447.RASPBERRY RIPPLE:

Time: 10 mins

Servings: 2

INGREDIENTS:

- 1 cup of raspberries
- 1 cup of coconut milk
- 1 tbsp agave syrup

INSTRUCTIONS:

1. Raspberries, coconut milk, and agave syrup Must all be put in a blender.

2. Blend everything thoroughly up to it's smooth.

3. Enjoy after pouring into serving glasses.

NUTRITION PER SERVING:

Cals: 120

Protein: 2g

Fat: 6g

Carbs: 14g

448.CREAMSICLE CREAMINESS:

Time: 10 mins

Servings: 2

INGREDIENTS:

- 1 cup of orange juice
- 1 cup of vanilla yogurt
- 1 tbsp honey

INSTRUCTIONS:

1. Orange juice, vanilla yogurt, and honey Must all be put in a blender.

2. Blend till creamy and smooth.

3. Pour cold liquid into glasses and serve.

NUTRITION PER SERVING:

Cals: 160

Protein: 6g

Fat: 2g

Carbs: 32g

449.KIWI KISS:

Time: 10 mins

Servings: 2

INGREDIENTS:

- 2 kiwis, peel off and diced
- 1 cup of spinach
- 1 cup of coconut water
- 1 tbsp lime juice
- 1 tsp honey (non-compulsory)

INSTRUCTIONS:

1. Kiwis, spinach, coconut water, lime juice, and honey Must all be mixd in a blender.

2. Blend everything thoroughly up to it's smooth.

3. Enjoy after pouring into serving glasses.

NUTRITION PER SERVING:

Cals: 90

Protein: 2g

Fat: 1g

Carbs: 20g

450.PEAR PLEASURE:

Time: 10 mins

Servings: 2

INGREDIENTS:

- 2 ripe pears, peel off and chop-up
- 1 cup of almond milk

- 1 tbsp almond butter
- 1 tsp maple syrup

INSTRUCTIONS:

1. Pears, almond milk, almond butter, and maple syrup are all mixd in a blender.

2. Blend till creamy and smooth.

3. Pour cold liquid into glasses and serve.

NUTRITION PER SERVING:

Cals: 180

Protein: 3g

Fat: 6g

Carbs: 30g

451.PEVERYY PASSION:

Time: 10 mins

Servings: 2

INGREDIENTS:

- 2 ripe peveryes, peel off and split
- 1 cup of Greek yogurt
- 1 tbsp agave syrup

INSTRUCTIONS:

1. Peveryes, Greek yogurt, and agave syrup are mixd in a blender.

2. Blend everything thoroughly up to it's smooth.

3. Enjoy after pouring into serving glasses.

NUTRITION PER SERVING:

Cals: 140

Protein: 12g

Fat: 2g

Carbs: 24g

452.STRAWBERRY SWIRL:

Time: 10 mins

Servings: 2

INGREDIENTS:

- 1 cup of strawberries
- 1 cup of coconut milk
- 1 tbsp honey

INSTRUCTIONS:

1. Strawberries, coconut milk, and honey Must all be mixd in a blender.

2. Blend till creamy and smooth.

3. Pour cold liquid into glasses and serve.

NUTRITION PER SERVING:

Cals: 130

Protein: 2g

Fat: 8g

Carbs: 16g

453.MELON MEDLEY:

Time: 10 mins

Servings: 2

INGREDIENTS:

- 1 cup of diced watermelon
- 1 cup of diced cantaloupe
- 1 cup of diced honeydew melon
- 1 tbsp lime juice

INSTRUCTIONS:

1. Watermelon, cantaloupe, honeydew melon, and lime juice Must all be mixd in a blender.

2. Blend everything thoroughly up to it's smooth.

3. Enjoy after pouring into serving glasses.

NUTRITION PER SERVING:

Cals: 80

Protein: 1g

Fat: 0g

Carbs: 20g

454.GOLDEN SUNSHINE:

Time: 15 mins

Servings: 2

INGREDIENTS:

- 2 oranges, peel off and segmented
- 1 cup of pineapple chunks
- 1 cup of coconut water
- 1 tbsp lemon juice
- 1 tsp turmeric powder

INSTRUCTIONS:

1. Oranges, pineapple chunks, coconut water, lemon juice, and turmeric powder Must all be mixd in a blender.

2. Blend everything thoroughly up to it's smooth.

3. Enjoy after pouring into serving glasses.

NUTRITION PER SERVING:

Cals: 120

Protein: 2g

Fat: 0g

Carbs: 30g

455. MINT MOJITO:

Time: 5 mins

Servings: 1

INGREDIENTS:

- 10 fresh mint leaves
- 2 tsp sugar
- 1 lime, juiced
- Ice cubes
- Club soda

INSTRUCTIONS:

1. Mint leaves, sugar, and lime juice Must be muddled in a glass up to the aroma of the leaves is released.
2. Ice cubes Must be put in the glass.
3. Add club soda on top, stirring well.
4. Serve after adding a mint sprig as a garnish.

456. GREEN REVIVAL:

Time: 5 mins

Servings: 1

INGREDIENTS:

- 1 cup of spinach
- 1 cup of kale
- 1 green apple, cored and chop-up
- 1/2 cucumber, chop-up
- 1/2 lemon, juiced
- 1 tbsp honey
- 1 cup of water

INSTRUCTIONS:

1. Blend spinach, kale, cucumber, green apple, lemon juice, honey, and water together in a blender.
2. Blend everything thoroughly up to it's smooth.
3. Pour cold liquid into a glass and serve.

457.BERRY BOOST:

Time: 5 mins

Servings: 1

INGREDIENTS:

- 1 cup of combined berries (strawberries, blueberries, raspberries)
- 1/2 cup of Greek yogurt
- 1/2 cup of almond milk
- 1 tbsp honey
- Ice cubes

INSTRUCTIONS:

1. Blend the combined berries, Greek yogurt, almond milk, honey, and ice cubes together in a blender.
2. Blend till creamy and smooth.
3. Pour cold liquid into a glass and serve.

458.CITRUS SYMPHONY:

Time: 5 mins

Servings: 1

INGREDIENTS:

- 1 orange, peel off and segmented
- 1 grapefruit, peel off and segmented
- 1 lemon, juiced
- 1 tsp honey
- Ice cubes

1. Orange and grapefruit segments, honey, lemon juice, and ice cubes Must all be put in a blender.
2. Blend everything thoroughly up to it's smooth.
3. Pour cold liquid into a glass and serve.

459.VEGGIE DELIGHT:

Time: 5 mins

Servings: 1

INGREDIENTS:

- 1 carrot, peel off and chop-up
- 1 celery stalk, chop-up
- 1/2 cucumber, chop-up
- 1/2 lemon, juiced
- 1/4 tsp salt
- 1/4 tsp black pepper
- Ice cubes

INSTRUCTIONS:

1. Mix cucumber, carrot, celery, lemon juice, salt, black pepper, and ice cubes in a blender.
2. Blend everything thoroughly up to it's smooth.
3. Pour cold liquid into a glass and serve.

460.POWER POTION:

Time: 5 mins

Servings: 1

INGREDIENTS:

- 1 cup of almond milk
- 1 banana
- 1 tbsp peanut butter
- 1 tbsp honey

- 1/2 tsp vanilla extract
- Ice cubes

INSTRUCTIONS:

1. Almond milk, a banana, peanut butter, honey, vanilla essence, and ice cubes Must all be blended together.
2. Blend till creamy and smooth.
3. Pour cold liquid into a glass and serve.

461.RAINBOW RIOT:

Time: 5 mins

Servings: 1

INGREDIENTS:

- 1/2 cup of pineapple chunks
- 1/2 cup of mango chunks
- 1/2 cup of strawberries
- 1/2 cup of blueberries
- 1/2 cup of coconut water
- Ice cubes

INSTRUCTIONS:

1. Strawberries, blueberries, pineapple pieces, mango chunks, coconut water, and ice cubes Must all be mixd in a blender.
2. Blend everything thoroughly up to it's smooth.
3. Pour cold liquid into a glass and serve.

462.LEMON LIME FUSION:

Time: 5 mins

Servings: 1

INGREDIENTS:

- 1 lemon, juiced
- 1 lime, juiced
- 1 tbsp sugar
- 1 cup of sparkling water
- Ice cubes

INSTRUCTIONS:

1. Mix sugar, lime juice, and lemon juice in a glass.
2. Stir the sugar up to it dissolves.
3. Ice cubes Must be added to the glass before sparkling water is added on top.
4. Stir thoroughly, then serve cold.

463.ORANGE OASIS:

Time: 5 mins

Servings: 1

INGREDIENTS:

- 1 orange, peel off and juiced
- 1/2 cup of coconut milk
- 1 tbsp agave nectar
- Ice cubes

INSTRUCTIONS:

1. Orange juice, coconut milk, agave nectar, and ice cubes Must all be blended together.
2. Blend till creamy and smooth.
3. Pour cold liquid into a glass and serve.

464.CARROT CRAZE:

Time: 5 mins

Servings: 1

INGREDIENTS:

- 1 carrot, peel off and juiced
- 1 apple, cored and juiced
- 1/2 lemon, juiced
- 1 tbsp ginger juice
- 1 tbsp honey
- Ice cubes

INSTRUCTIONS:

1. Juices from carrots, apples, lemons, gingers, honey, and ice cubes are mixd in a blender.
2. Blend everything thoroughly.
3. Pour cold liquid into a glass and serve.

465.BEETROOT BLISS

Time: 10 mins

Servings: 2

INGREDIENTS:

- 1 medium beetroot, peel off and chop-up
- 1 cup of strawberries, hulled
- 1 cup of orange juice
- 1 tbsp honey (non-compulsory)
- Ice cubes

INSTRUCTIONS:

1. Beetroot, strawberries, orange juice, and honey (if using) Must all be mixd in a blender.

2. Blend everything thoroughly up to it's smooth.

3. When the mixture is cold and foamy, add ice cubes and mix once more.

4. Pour into glasses and start serving right away.

NUTRITION INFO (PER SERVING):

Cals: 120

Protein: 3g

Fat: 0.5g

Carbs: 28g

Fiber: 4g

466.PINEAPPLE PARADISE

Time: 5 mins

Servings: 1

INGREDIENTS:

- 1 cup of fresh pineapple chunks
- 1/2 cup of coconut milk
- 1/2 cup of orange juice
- 1 tbsp lime juice
- 1 tbsp honey (non-compulsory)
- Ice cubes

INSTRUCTIONS:

1. Blend the pineapple chunks, coconut milk, lime, orange, and honey (if used) in a blender.

2. Blend till creamy and smooth.

3. When the mixture is cold and foamy, add ice cubes and mix once more.

4. Place in a glass and sip.

Cals: 180

Protein: 1g

Fat: 5g

Carbs: 40g

Fiber: 2g

467.MANGO MAGIC

Time: 5 mins

Servings: 1

INGREDIENTS:

- 1 ripe mango, peel off and diced
- 1/2 cup of Greek yogurt
- 1/2 cup of orange juice
- 1 tbsp honey (non-compulsory)
- Ice cubes

INSTRUCTIONS:

1. Mango dice, Greek yogurt, orange juice, and honey (if used) Must all be mixd in a blender.

2. Blend till creamy and smooth.

3. When the mixture is cold and foamy, add ice cubes and mix once more.

4. Pour into a glass, then serve right away.

NUTRITION INFO (PER SERVING):

Cals: 220

Protein: 8g

Fat: 2g

Carbs: 46g

Fiber: 4g

468.WATERMELON WHIRL

Time: 5 mins

Servings: 2

INGREDIENTS:

- 2 cups of seedless watermelon, cubed
- 1/2 cup of fresh mint leaves
- 1 tbsp lime juice
- 1 tbsp honey (non-compulsory)
- Ice cubes

INSTRUCTIONS:

1. Watermelon cubes, mint leaves, lime juice, and honey (if using) Must all be mixd in a blender.

2. Blend everything thoroughly up to it's smooth.

3. When the mixture is cold and foamy, add ice cubes and mix once more.

4. Pour into glasses and start serving right away.

NUTRITION INFO (PER SERVING):

Cals: 70

Protein: 1g

Fat: 0g

Carbs: 18g

Fiber: 1g

469.GINGER SPICE

Time: 10 mins

Servings: 1

INGREDIENTS:

- 1 inch fresh ginger, peel off and finely grated
- 1 cup of apple juice
- 1 tbsp lemon juice
- 1 tbsp honey (non-compulsory)
- Ice cubes

INSTRUCTIONS:

1. Finely grated ginger, apple juice, lemon juice, and honey (if using) Must all be blended together.

2. Blend everything thoroughly.

3. When the mixture is cold and foamy, add ice cubes and mix once more.

4. Place in a glass and sip.

NUTRITION INFO (PER SERVING):

Cals: 90

Protein: 0g

Fat: 0g

Carbs: 24g

Fiber: 0g

470.POMEGRANATE POTION

Time: 10 mins

Servings: 2

INGREDIENTS:

- 1 cup of pomegranate seeds
- 1/2 cup of cranberry juice
- 1/2 cup of orange juice
- 1 tbsp lime juice
- 1 tbsp honey (non-compulsory)
- Ice cubes

INSTRUCTIONS:

1. Pomegranate seeds, cranberry juice, orange juice, lime juice, and honey (if using) Must all be mixd in a blender.

2. Blend everything thoroughly up to it's smooth.

3. When the mixture is cold and foamy, add ice cubes and mix once more.

4. Pour into glasses and start serving right away.

NUTRITION INFO (PER SERVING):

Cals: 100

Protein: 1g

Fat: 0g

Carbs: 25g

Fiber: 2g

471. BLUEBERRY BURST

Time: 5 mins

Servings: 1

INGREDIENTS:

- 1 cup of fresh blueberries
- 1/2 cup of almond milk
- 1/2 cup of Greek yogurt
- 1 tbsp honey (non-compulsory)
- Ice cubes

INSTRUCTIONS:

1. Blend the blueberries, almond milk, Greek yogurt, and honey (if using) together in a blender.

2. Blend till creamy and smooth.

3. When the mixture is cold and foamy, add ice cubes and mix once more.

4. Place in a glass and sip.

NUTRITION INFO (PER SERVING):

Cals: 150

Protein: 6g

Fat: 2g

Carbs: 29g

Fiber: 4g

472.RASPBERRY RHAPSODY

Time: 5 mins

Servings: 1

INGREDIENTS:

- 1 cup of fresh raspberries
- 1/2 cup of coconut water
- 1/2 cup of pineapple juice
- 1 tbsp honey (non-compulsory)
- Ice cubes

INSTRUCTIONS:

1. Blend the raspberries, coconut water, pineapple juice, and honey (if using) together in a blender.

2. Blend everything thoroughly up to it's smooth.

3. When the mixture is cold and foamy, add ice cubes and mix once more.

4. Pour into a glass, then serve right away.

NUTRITION INFO (PER SERVING):

Cals: 120

Protein: 1g

Fat: 1g

Carbs: 29g

Fiber: 8g

473.CREAMY CITRUS

Time: 5 mins

Servings: 1

INGREDIENTS:

- 1 orange, peel off
- 1/2 cup of plain Greek yogurt
- 1/4 cup of almond milk
- 1 tbsp honey (non-compulsory)
- Ice cubes

INSTRUCTIONS:

1. Orange, Greek yogurt, almond milk, and honey (if using) Must all be blended together.

2. Blend till creamy and smooth.

3. When the mixture is cold and foamy, add ice cubes and mix once more.

4. Place in a glass and sip.

NUTRITION INFO (PER SERVING):

Cals: 150

Protein: 9g

Fat: 2g

Carbs: 28g

Fiber: 4g

474.KIWI DELIGHT

Time: 5 mins

Servings: 1

INGREDIENTS:

- 2 ripe kiwis, peel off and diced
- 1/2 cup of coconut water
- 1/2 cup of pineapple juice
- 1 tbsp lime juice
- 1 tbsp honey (non-compulsory)
- Ice cubes

INSTRUCTIONS:

1. The split kiwis, coconut water, pineapple juice, lime juice, and honey (if used) Must all be mixd in a blender.

2. Blend everything thoroughly up to it's smooth.

3. When the mixture is cold and foamy, add ice cubes and mix once more.

4. Pour into a glass, then serve right away.

NUTRITION INFO (PER SERVING):

Cals: 140

Protein: 2g

Fat: 0.5g

Carbs: 35g

Fiber: 5g

475. PEAR PARADISE:

Time: 5 mins

Servings: 1

INGREDIENTS:

- 1 ripe pear
- 1 cup of almond milk
- 1 tbsp honey
- 1/2 tsp vanilla extract
- Ice cubes (non-compulsory)

INSTRUCTIONS:

1. The pear Must be peel off, cored, and then slice into pieces.
2. Blend the pear pieces, almond milk, honey, and vanilla essence in a blender.
3. Blend till creamy and smooth.
4. If preferred, include a few ice cubes and blend once more up to thoroughly incorporated.
5. Pour into a glass, then sip.

476. PEVERY PERFECTION:

Time: 10 mins

Servings: 2

INGREDIENTS:

- 2 ripe peveryes
- 1 cup of Greek yogurt
- 1/2 cup of orange juice
- 1 tbsp honey
- 1/2 tsp cinnamon
- Ice cubes (non-compulsory)

INSTRUCTIONS:

1. The peveryes Must be peel off, pitted, and then slice into pieces.

2. The pevery chunks, Greek yogurt, orange juice, honey, and cinnamon Must all be mixd in a blender.
3. Blend till creamy and smooth.
4. If preferred, include a few ice cubes and blend once more up to thoroughly incorporated.
5. Pour cold liquid into glasses and serve.

477.STRAWBERRY SMOOTHIE:

Time: 5 mins

Servings: 1

INGREDIENTS:

- 1 cup of fresh or refrigerate strawberries
- 1/2 cup of milk (dairy or plant-based)
- 1/2 cup of plain yogurt
- 1 tbsp honey or maple syrup
- 1/2 tsp vanilla extract
- Ice cubes (non-compulsory)

INSTRUCTIONS:

1. Blend together the strawberries, yogurt, milk, honey, or maple syrup, and vanilla extract.
2. Blend till creamy and smooth.
3. If preferred, include a few ice cubes and blend once more up to thoroughly incorporated.
4. To serve, pour into a glass.

478.MELON MANIA:

Time: 10 mins

Servings: 2

INGREDIENTS:

- 2 cups of diced combined melons (watermelon, cantaloupe, honeydew)
- 1/2 cup of coconut water
- 1 tbsp lime juice
- 1 tbsp fresh mint leaves
- Ice cubes (non-compulsory)

INSTRUCTIONS:

1. Mix the chop-up combined melon, lime juice, coconut water, and fresh mint leaves in a combiner.
2. Blend everything thoroughly up to it's smooth.
3. Add some ice cubes if desired, then blend again up to cooled.
4. Pour into glasses and, if preferred, top with more mint leaves.

479.GOLDEN ELIXIR:

Time: 5 mins

Servings: 1

INGREDIENTS:

- 1 ripe banana
- 1 cup of coconut water
- 1 tbsp turmeric powder
- 1 tbsp honey or maple syrup
- 1/2 tsp ginger powder
- Ice cubes (non-compulsory)

INSTRUCTIONS:

1. Bananas Must be peel off and slice into pieces.

2. Banana chunks, coconut water, ginger powder, honey, or maple syrup, and turmeric powder Must all be blended together.
3. Blend up to well-mixd and smooth.
4. Add some ice cubes if desired, then blend again up to cooled.
5. Pour into a glass, then sip.

480.MINT MARVEL:

Time: 5 mins

Servings: 1

INGREDIENTS:

- 1 cup of spinach
- 1 cup of pineapple chunks
- 1/2 cup of coconut milk
- 1 tbsp fresh mint leaves
- 1 tbsp lime juice
- Ice cubes (non-compulsory)

INSTRUCTIONS:

1. Blend the spinach, pineapple pieces, coconut milk, lime juice, and fresh mint leaves together in a blender.
2. Blend everything thoroughly up to it's smooth.
3. Add some ice cubes if desired, then blend again up to cooled.
4. To serve, pour into a glass.

481. GREEN GARDEN:

Time: 10 mins

Servings: 2

INGREDIENTS:

- 2 cups of combined greens (spinach, kale, arugula)
- 1 cup of cucumber, chop-up
- 1 ripe avocado, pitted and peel off
- 1/2 cup of green apple, chop-up
- 1 tbsp lemon juice
- 1 cup of coconut water
- Ice cubes (non-compulsory)

INSTRUCTIONS:

1. The combined greens, cucumber, avocado, green apple, lemon juice, and coconut water Must all be mixd in a blender.
2. Blend thoroughly and smoothly.
3. Add some ice cubes if desired, then blend again up to cooled.
4. Pour into glasses, then offer.

482. BERRY BOOST:

Time: 5 mins

Servings: 1

INGREDIENTS:

- 1 cup of combined berries (strawberries, blueberries, raspberries)
- 1/2 cup of almond milk
- 1/2 cup of plain Greek yogurt
- 1 tbsp honey or maple syrup
- 1/2 tsp chia seeds
- Ice cubes (non-compulsory)

INSTRUCTIONS:

1. The combined berries, almond milk, Greek yogurt, honey, or maple syrup, and chia seeds Must all be put in a blender.
2. Blend everything thoroughly up to it's smooth.
3. Add some ice cubes if desired, then blend again up to cooled.
4. Pour into a glass, then sip.

483.CITRUS DELIGHT:

Time: 5 mins

Servings: 1

INGREDIENTS:

- 1 orange, peel off and segmented
- 1 grapefruit, peel off and segmented
- 1/2 cup of pineapple chunks
- 1/2 cup of coconut water
- 1 tbsp lime juice
- Ice cubes (non-compulsory)

INSTRUCTIONS:

1. Orange and grapefruit segments, pineapple chunks, coconut water, and lime juice Must all be mixd in a blender.
2. Blend thoroughly and smoothly.
3. Add some ice cubes if desired, then blend again up to cooled.
4. To serve, pour into a glass.

484.VEGGIE HEAVEN:

Time: 10 mins

Servings: 2

INGREDIENTS:

- 2 medium carrots, chop-up
- 1 cucumber, chop-up
- 1 stalk celery, chop-up
- 1 cup of baby spinach
- 1/2 cup of coconut water
- 1 tbsp lemon juice
- Ice cubes (non-compulsory)

INSTRUCTIONS:

1. The diced carrots, cucumber, celery, baby spinach, coconut water, and lemon juice Must all be mixd in a blender.
2. Blend everything thoroughly up to it's smooth.
3. Add some ice cubes if desired, then blend again up to cooled.
4. Pour into glasses, then offer.

485.POWER BLEND:

Time: 5 mins

Servings: 2

INGREDIENTS:

- 1 cup of spinach
- 1 ripe banana
- 1/2 cup of almond milk
- 1 tbsp chia seeds
- 1 tbsp honey

INSTRUCTIONS:

1. Blend the spinach, banana, almond milk, chia seeds, and honey in a blender.

2. Blend till creamy and smooth.

3. Pour into glasses and start serving right away.

NUTRITION INFO:

Cals: 180

Protein: 4g

Fat: 4g

Carbs: 35g

Fiber: 6g

486.RAINBOW SPLASH:

Time: 10 mins

Servings: 4

INGREDIENTS:

- 1 cup of strawberries
- 1/2 cup of pineapple chunks
- 1/2 cup of blueberries
- 1/2 cup of chop-up kiwi
- 1/2 cup of mango chunks
- 1 cup of coconut water
- 1 tbsp lime juice

INSTRUCTIONS:

1. Strawberries, pineapple pieces, blueberries, kiwi, mango chunks, coconut water, and lime juice Must all be mixd in a blender.

2. Up to smooth, blend.

3. Pour cold liquid into glasses and serve.

NUTRITION INFO:

Cals: 80

Protein: 1g

Fat: 0g

Carbs: 20g

Fiber: 4g

487.LEMONADE TWIST:

Time: 15 mins

Servings: 6

INGREDIENTS:

- 6 lemons
- 1/2 cup of honey
- 6 cups of cold water
- Ice cubes
- Lemon slices (for garnish)

INSTRUCTIONS:

1. Juice the lemons, then drain it to get rid of any pulp or seeds.

2. Lemon juice, honey, and cold water Must all be mixd in a pitcher. The honey must be well dissolved, so stir well.

3. Lemon slices are used as a garnish after adding ice cubes to the pitcher.

4. Offer cold.

NUTRITION INFO:

Cals: 80

Protein: 0g

Fat: 0g

Carbs: 23g

Fiber: 0g

488.ORANGE DELIGHT:

Time: 5 mins

Servings: 2

INGREDIENTS:

- 2 oranges
- 1/2 cup of Greek yogurt
- 1 tbsp honey
- Ice cubes

INSTRUCTIONS:

1. Oranges Must be seedless and peel off.

2. Blend the oranges, Greek yogurt, honey, and ice cubes together in a blender.

3. Blend till creamy and smooth.

4. Pour cold liquid into glasses and serve.

NUTRITION INFO:

Cals: 120

Protein: 6g

Fat: 0g

Carbs: 26g

Fiber: 4g

489.CARROT COOLER:

Time: 10 mins

Servings: 2

INGREDIENTS:

- 2 Big carrots
- 1 apple
- 1/2 inch fresh ginger
- 1 tbsp lemon juice
- Ice cubes

INSTRUCTIONS:

1. Apple and carrots Must be peel off and slice into mini pieces.

2. Mix the carrots, apple, ginger, lemon juice, and ice cubes in a blender.

3. Up to smooth, blend.

4. Pour cold liquid into glasses and serve.

NUTRITION INFO:

Cals: 90

Protein: 2g

Fat: 0g

Carbs: 22g

Fiber: 4g

490.BEETROOT BEAUTY:

Time: 10 mins

Servings: 2

INGREDIENTS:

- 1 Big beetroot
- 1 apple
- 1/2 cup of Greek yogurt
- 1 tbsp honey
- Ice cubes

INSTRUCTIONS:

1. The apple and beetroot Must be peel off and slice into mini pieces.

2. Blend the beets, apple, Greek yogurt, honey, and ice cubes in a blender.

3. Blend till creamy and smooth.

4. Pour cold liquid into glasses and serve.

NUTRITION INFO:

Cals: 150

Protein: 6g

Fat: 0g

Carbs: 30g

Fiber: 5g

491.PINEAPPLE PASSION:

Time: 5 mins

Servings: 2

INGREDIENTS:

- 1 cup of chop-up pineapple
- 1/2 cup of coconut milk
- 1/2 cup of orange juice
- 1 tbsp lime juice
- Ice cubes

INSTRUCTIONS:

1. The chop-up pineapple, coconut milk, lime juice, orange juice, and ice cubes Must all be blended together.

2. Up to smooth, blend.

3. Pour cold liquid into glasses and serve.

NUTRITION INFO:

Cals: 120

Protein: 1g

Fat: 6g

Carbs: 20g

Fiber: 2g

492.MANGO MARVEL:

Time: 5 mins

Servings: 2

INGREDIENTS:

- 1 ripe mango
- 1 cup of coconut water
- 1/2 cup of orange juice
- Ice cubes

INSTRUCTIONS:

1. The ripe mango Must be peel off and slice into mini pieces.

2. Mango, coconut water, orange juice, and ice cubes Must all be blended together.

3. Blend till creamy and smooth.

4. Pour cold liquid into glasses and serve.

NUTRITION INFO:

Cals: 150

Protein: 2g

Fat: 1g

Carbs: 38g

Fiber: 3g

493.WATERMELON CRUSH:

Time: 10 mins

Servings: 4

INGREDIENTS:

- 4 cups of cubed watermelon
- 1 tbsp fresh mint leaves
- 1 tbsp lime juice
- Ice cubes

INSTRUCTIONS:

1. The cubed watermelon, fresh mint leaves, lime juice, and ice cubes Must all be blended together.

2. Up to smooth, blend.

3. Pour cold liquid into glasses and serve.

NUTRITION INFO:

Cals: 45

Protein: 1g

Fat: 0g

Carbs: 11g

Fiber: 1g

494.GINGER FIRE:

Time: 10 mins

Servings: 2

INGREDIENTS:

- 1 inch fresh ginger
- 2 oranges
- 1 tbsp honey
- 1 cup of cold water
- Ice cubes

INSTRUCTIONS:

1. Fresh ginger Must be peel off and slice into mini pieces.

2. Oranges Must be juiced, and any pulp or seeds Must be filtered out.

3. Ginger that has been diced, orange juice, honey, cold water, and ice cubes Must all be put in a blender.

4. Blend everything thoroughly.

5. Pour cold liquid into glasses and serve.

NUTRITION INFO:

Cals: 70

Protein: 1g

Fat: 0g

Carbs: 18g

Fiber: 1g

495.POMEGRANATE PUNCH:

Time: 10 mins

Servings: 4

INGREDIENTS:

- 2 cups of pomegranate juice
- 1 cup of orange juice
- 1/4 cup of lemon juice
- 1/4 cup of lime juice
- 2 tbsp honey
- 1 cup of sparkling water
- Ice cubes
- Mint leaves (for garnish)

INSTRUCTIONS:

1. Pomegranate juice, orange juice, lemon juice, lime juice, and honey Must all be mixd in a pitcher.
2. Up to the honey is dissolved, stir thoroughly.
3. Gently stir in the sparkling water.
4. Garnish with mint leaves before serving over ice cubes.

496.BLUEBERRY BLAST:

Time: 5 mins

Servings: 2

INGREDIENTS:

- 1 cup of blueberries
- 1 cup of vanilla yogurt
- 1/2 cup of milk
- 1 tbsp honey
- Ice cubes

INSTRUCTIONS:

1. The blueberries, vanilla yogurt, milk, and honey Must all be put in a blender.
2. Blend till creamy and smooth.
3. Once you've gotten the correct consistency, add ice cubes and blend once more.
4. Pour into glasses and start serving right away.

497.RASPBERRY RAPTURE:

Time: 5 mins

Servings: 2

INGREDIENTS:

- 1 cup of raspberries
- 1 cup of coconut water
- 1/2 cup of pineapple juice
- 1 tbsp lime juice
- Ice cubes
- Fresh raspberries (for garnish)

INSTRUCTIONS:

1. Blend the raspberries, coconut water, pineapple juice, and lime juice together in a blender.
2. Up to smooth, blend.
3. Blend again while adding ice cubes up to thoroughly blended.
4. Serve with fresh raspberries as a garnish after pouring into glasses.

498.CREAMY COCONUT:

Time: 5 mins

Servings: 2

INGREDIENTS:

- 1 cup of coconut milk
- 1 ripe banana
- 1/2 cup of pineapple chunks

- 1 tbsp honey
- Ice cubes
- Shredded coconut (for garnish)

INSTRUCTIONS:

1. Blend the coconut milk, chunks of pineapple, ripe banana, and honey together in a blender.
2. Blend till creamy and smooth.
3. Blend again while adding ice cubes up to thoroughly blended.
4. Pour into glasses, top with coconut shreds, and serve.

499.KIWI FUSION:

Time: 5 mins

Servings: 2

INGREDIENTS:

- 2 ripe kiwis
- 1 cup of green grapes
- 1/2 cup of apple juice
- 1 tbsp lime juice
- Ice cubes
- Kiwi slices (for garnish)

INSTRUCTIONS:

1. The ripe kiwis, green grapes, apple juice, and lime juice Must all be mixd in a blender.
2. Up to smooth, blend.
3. Blend again while adding ice cubes up to thoroughly blended.
4. Pour into glasses, add kiwi slices as a garnish, and then serve.

500.PEAR PERK:

Time: 5 mins

Servings: 2

INGREDIENTS:

- 2 ripe pears
- 1 cup of spinach leaves
- 1/2 cup of almond milk
- 1 tbsp honey
- Ice cubes
- Fresh mint leaves (for garnish)

INSTRUCTIONS:

1. Blend the ripe pears, spinach leaves, almond milk, and honey in a blender.
2. Up to smooth, blend.
3. Blend again while adding ice cubes up to thoroughly blended.
4. Add liquid to glasses, top with mint leaves, and serve.

501PEVERYY PLEASURE:

Time: 5 mins

Servings: 2

INGREDIENTS:

- 2 ripe peveryes
- 1 cup of orange juice
- 1/2 cup of Greek yogurt
- 1 tbsp honey
- Ice cubes
- Pevery slices (for garnish)

INSTRUCTIONS:

1. The ripe peveryes, orange juice, Greek yogurt, and honey Must all be mixd in a blender.

2. Blend till creamy and smooth.
3. Blend again while adding ice cubes up to thoroughly blended.
4. Pour into glasses, add pevery slices as a garnish, and then serve.

502.STRAWBERRY DELIGHT:

Time: 5 mins

Servings: 2

INGREDIENTS:

- 1 cup of strawberries
- 1 cup of milk
- 1/2 cup of vanilla ice cream
- 1 tbsp honey
- Ice cubes
- Fresh strawberries (for garnish)

INSTRUCTIONS:

1. Strawberries, milk, vanilla ice cream, and honey Must all be blended together.
2. Blend till creamy and smooth.
3. Blend again while adding ice cubes up to thoroughly blended.
4. Serve after pouring into glasses and adding fresh strawberries as a garnish.

Printed in Great Britain
by Amazon

29018712R00236